Financial Wisdom English

金融英语阅读与听力训练 ○ 附光盘

金融睿智英语

沈素萍／系列主编

1 世界金融名家
World Financial Celebrities

茅海红／编著

中国金融出版社

责任编辑：肖　炜
责任校对：刘　明
责任印制：程　颖

图书在版编目（CIP）数据

世界金融名家（Shijie Jinrong Mingjia）：汉英对照/茅海红编著．—北京：
中国金融出版社，2009.10
（金融睿智英语/沈素萍系列主编）
ISBN 978 - 7 - 5049 - 4874 - 8

Ⅰ．世…　Ⅱ．茅…　Ⅲ．①英语—汉语—对照读物 ②金融家—生平事
迹—世界　Ⅳ．H319.4：K

中国版本图书馆 CIP 数据核字（2008）第 174808 号

出版
发行　中国金融出版社

社址　北京市丰台区益泽路 2 号
市场开发部　（010）63272190，66070804（传真）
网上书店　http://www.chinafph.com
　　　　　（010）63286832，63365686（传真）
读者服务部　（010）66070833，82672183
邮编　100071
经销　新华书店
印刷　北京松源印刷有限公司
尺寸　169 毫米 × 239 毫米
印张　15.75
字数　282 千
版次　2009 年 10 月第 1 版
印次　2009 年 10 月第 1 次印刷
定价　35.00 元
ISBN 978 - 7 - 5049 - 4874 - 8/F. 4434
如出现印装错误本社负责调换　联系电话（010）63263947

在金融英语的教学生涯中，笔者编写了不同层次和侧重点的金融英语教材二十余部，此次《金融睿智英语》系列丛书的策划，是应中国金融出版社孟威锋主任的邀请，编写有关金融英语听力方面的教材，正值笔者受邀到美国哈佛大学参与研究，所以，结合做中外银行历史体制的比较，最后确定编写一套了解金融历史的发展过程并兼顾英语语言学习的丛书。

本套系列丛书题材广泛，涵盖了一些不同类型的专题。首先在《世界金融名家》（World Financial Celebrities）中我们选择了银行家、诺贝尔奖获得者、投资大师、证券分析家等金融界杰出人物。其次在《金融危机》（Financial Crisis）中我们沿着历史上全球金融危机典型案例的轨迹来介绍金融历史。其中有17世纪荷兰的郁金香泡沫事件（Tulip Mania），18世纪英国的南海泡沫事件（South Sea Bubble），1929年美国经济大萧条（Great Depression）以及1997年的亚洲金融风暴（Asian Financial Crisis）。特别是2008年9月雷曼兄弟公司破产（Bankruptcy of Lehman Brothers）成为美国历史上最大的倒闭案件。另外，本套丛书还包括金融改革、法律、电子金融、银行管理、金融人物励志案例等专题。

本系列读物均按照由浅入深、循序渐进的原则系统而连贯地编写完成。每册各自在内容上互相渗透，融会贯通。同时，每册又各具特色，风格迥异。

本套丛书语言设计新颖。每册编写共分20个单元左右，每个单元分七个部分："主题札记"、"阅读长廊"、"财经宝库"、"DIY工作室"、"归类记忆卡片"、"听力广场"和"非常点拨"。另外，丛书的语言生动活泼。"主题札记"是每单元的导读部分。我们用中文简单介绍本单元所要谈及的主题，便于读者阅读和进行听力学习。我们又在英文全文后加入了对应的中文翻译，并配有相关的人物照片及事件图例，让读者在轻松活泼的氛围中了解金融。同时，我们也注重语言设计的严谨。"阅读长廊"是一个单元的主要部分，采取中英文对照方式，同时对于生词采用脚注方式，标明音标、词性和文中含义。"财经宝库"主要针对文中涉及的与金融知识相关的词条做注释，方便读者直观快速了解金融背景知识。"DIY工作室"针对阅读材料提问题，便于读者思考总结。"听力广场"以中英文对照方式出现，其中的难点还在"非常点拨"中做了注释。

这套丛书可作为系列金融英语读物和教材（含配套听力光盘），

旨在帮助金融专业学生和金融从业人员在了解金融专业知识的同时，提高金融英语听说和阅读能力。在丛书的策划和出版过程中，中国金融出版社的孟威锋主任和肖炜、杨敏编辑为我们提供了很多宝贵的建议，在此谨致谢忱。

系列主编　沈素萍
2009年5月于哈佛园

作为中国金融出版社《金融睿智英语》系列丛书的首篇作品，《世界金融名家》精心遴选全球具有代表性的十八位金融名家，编写十八个单元，每个单元通过"主题札记"、"阅读长廊"、"财经宝库"、"DIY工作室"、"归类记忆卡片"、"听力广场"和"非常点拨"七个部分，介绍他们的传奇经历和投资理念。相关材料具有权威性，同时兼顾趣味性和难易程度。

这十八位金融名家都是国际经济和金融领域叱咤风云的人物，包括三位中国人物和十五位国际人物，如周小川、吉姆·罗杰斯、乔治·索罗斯、本·伯南克、沃伦·巴菲特、罗伯特·蒙代尔、约瑟夫·斯蒂格利茨等。他们之中有的是著名银行家，有的是投资高手，有的是经济学大师，有的是诺贝尔奖获得者；林林总总，不一而足。

编书的过程如同一次旅行，是将梦想付诸实践的一种经历，更是进一步学习的一个契机。这十八位金融名家中，每一位人物都有很多极富教益的故事。编写他们的材料，就如同与这些大师们的一次零距离接触。编者尽己所能，将最好的材料奉献给读者。希望我们能一起徜徉在阅读长廊中，聆听他们的神奇故事，品味他们的传奇经历。

编写此书时，正值举世瞩目的第29届奥林匹克运动会在北京召开。面对这样的历史时刻和书籍出版日期的压力，从繁忙的生活和工作中挤出时间搜集材料并进行编写，难度可想而知。在此，我要感谢《金融睿智英语》系列主编、正在美国哈佛大学做访问学者的沈素萍教授的信任和鼓励，也要感谢中国金融出版社孟威锋主任和肖炜编辑等的大力帮助，同时还要感谢家人的理解和支持。

书稿付梓之时正值世界金融危机肆虐之际。如果读者能从这些金融大师的经营策略和投资理念中得到一些启迪，更好地分析当前金融危机的原因和影响，对我们的生活和工作有些许助益，作者就喜不自禁了。

最后，欢迎读者对本书提出意见和建议，作者将认真听取并尽可能地加以改进。

茅海红

2009年5月于北京

Contents 目录

World Financial Celebrities

Ben Bernanke

Unit 1

Ben Bernanke
美联储的新当家：本·伯南克

主题札记

本·伯南克，1953年12月13日出生于美国佐治亚州的奥古斯塔。1975年获得哈佛大学经济学学士学位，1979年获得麻省理工学院博士学位。毕业后，他在美国顶尖学府普林斯顿大学任教，长期担任经济与公共事务管理教授，并做过6年的经济系主任。凭借敏锐的经济洞察力，伯南克赢得了华尔街的青睐。

2005年10月24日下午，美国总统布什在白宫宣布，美国中央银行，也就是美国联邦储备委员会（简称美联储）主席格林斯潘将于2006年1月31日卸任，由总统经济顾问委员会主席本·伯南克接掌其职。一时间，伯南克其人其事成为全世界媒体关注的焦点。控制通货膨胀率一直是美联储的核心职能。在过去的半个世纪里，美国只经历过5任美联储主席，他们的成功和失败均与通货膨胀率息息相关。

伯南克在担任美联储委员时，曾多次警告美国经济要提防通货紧缩的威胁，以免重蹈日本经济衰退的覆辙。在2002年11月的一次讲话中，伯南克暗示美联储将用一切手段遏制通货紧缩，甚至可以"大量印制钞票并用直升机散发"来鼓励消费。伯南克因此被冠以"超级鸽派"的称号。

阅读长廊

Ben Bernanke has a tough road to walk on

By Daniel McGinn and Richard Wolffe

Bernanke was born on December 13, 1953, in Augusta, Georgia, but grew up in Dillon, South Carolina. He is the eldest of three children, having a younger brother and sister. His father Philip was a pharmacist[1] and part-time theater manager, and his mother Edna was originally a school teacher. They were one of the few Jewish families in the area. As a child, Bernanke learned Hebrew from his maternal grandfather Harold Friedman.

Bernanke spent his undergraduate years at Harvard University and graduated with a B.A. in economics in 1975. He performed no military service. Throughout college, he worked as a waiter to support himself during the summer at

本·伯南克可谓任重而道远

伯南克1953年12月13日出生于美国佐治亚州的奥古斯塔，但他在南卡罗来纳州的狄龙长大。他是家里的长子，还有一个弟弟和一个妹妹。他的父亲菲利普是一名药剂师，兼职做剧院经理，他的母亲艾德娜原先是学校教师。他们是这个区少有的几个犹太家庭之一。在孩提时代，伯南克跟着他姥爷哈罗德·弗莱德曼学习希伯莱语。

伯南克在哈佛大学读本科，1975年获得哈佛大学经济学学士学位。他没有服兵役。为了自立，整个大学期间的暑假，他都在他的家乡狄龙的一个路边景点当服务生。

---

[1] pharmacist ['fɑ:məsist] n.药剂师

a roadside attraction in his hometown of Dillon. He received a Ph.D. in economics from the Massachusetts Institute of Technology in 1979.

Bernanke taught at the Stanford Graduate School of Business from 1979 until 1985, was a visiting professor at New York University and went on to become a tenured professor at Princeton University in the Department of Economics. Dr. Bernanke was a member of the Board of Governors of the Federal Reserve System from 2002 to 2005. On February 1, 2006, he was appointed as a member of the Board for a fourteen-year term and to a four-year term as Chairman.

Bernanke was raised in rural South Carolina. As a teenager, he worked briefly as a waiter at the South of the Border tourist trap on Interstate 95. Early on, says his father, Philip, the town's pharmacist, it was clear "he was destined for something greater than a small-town drugstore". At Harvard, he discovered economics and spent hours at a mainframe[2] computer, tinkering with natural-gas pricing models for his senior thesis. His advisor, Harvard economist Dale Jorgenson, noted the irony: when Jorgenson visited the Fed last month, natural-gas pricing was again a hot topic. As a doctoral student at MIT in

1979年他获得麻省理工学院经济学博士学位。

伯南克从1979年到1985年在斯坦福大学研究生院教书，也是纽约大学的客座教授，后来又成为普林斯顿大学经济学系的终身教授。从2002年到2005年，他担任联邦储备委员会理事。2006年2月1日，他被任命为任期14年的美联储委员和任期4年的美联储主席。

伯南克在南卡罗来纳州的农村地区长大。十几岁时，他曾在95号州际公路旁边一家名为"边境以南"的餐馆当过一阵子服务生。他那在镇上当药剂师的父亲菲利普说，很早时候就能看出，"儿子注定会成就一番伟业，而不是掌管小镇上的一家药店"。他在哈佛大学首次对经济学产生了兴趣，会在大型计算机前坐上几小时，研究天然气定价模型，以此作为毕业论文。他的指导老师，哈佛大学的经济学家戴尔·乔根森提到了这件颇有意思的事情：上个月，乔根森造访美联储时，天然气的定价再度成为一

---

[2] mainframe ['meinfreim] n.（尤指除外部辅助装置的）计算机

the late 1970s, Bernanke became focused on the causes of the Great Depression. After earning his Ph.D., he continued that research for a decade. "I guess I am a Great Depression buff [3], the way some people are Civil War buffs," he later wrote. "To understand the Great Depression is the Holy Grail[4] of macro-economics."

When Ben Bernanke left his post at the Federal Reserve last spring to become President George W. Bush's top economic advisor, his work pals didn't give him much of a send-off, Only a month ago did his Fed colleges get around to throwing him a lunchtime goodbye party. In keeping with Fed tradition, Bernanke's favorite food—Necco candy wafers[5]—was served, and the going-away gifts included a Steuben crystal eagle, a framed set of dollar bills and the chair Bernanke sat in during Fed meetings. This winter, however, Bernanke will need to deliver that chair back to the Fed— and perhaps return the going-away presents, too. After months of oddsmaking from Washington to Wall Street about who would succeed Federal Reserve chairman Alan Greenspan,79, when his term expires in January, last week Greenspan and Bernanke strode into the Oval Office for the announcement. After 18 years leading the Fed,

个热门话题。20世纪70年代末期，伯南克还在麻省理工学院攻读博士时，他就潜心研究导致经济大萧条的根源。获得博士学位后，他对这个课题继续研究了十年。他后来撰文道："我想我热衷于研究大萧条，就像有些人热衷于研究美国内战那样。弄清楚大萧条是宏观经济学梦寐以求的目标。"

当本·伯南克在去年春季离开在联邦储备委员会，成为布什总统首席经济顾问时，他的同仁并没有为他举办隆重的欢送会。只是在一个月之前，他在美联储的一群同仁抽出时间，在午餐时间为他举办了告别会。按照美联储的传统，端上来的是伯南克最爱吃的食物：新英格兰糖果公司生产的糖酥饼，其他离任礼物包括一座斯托伊本水晶鹰像、一套裱框起来的美元钞票，还有伯南克在美联储开会期间所坐的那把椅子。不过今年冬季，伯南克可能要把那把椅子运回美联储——其他离任礼物恐怕也要一并归还。近几个月来，华盛顿到华尔街的人士一直在猜测谁会接任将在明年1月卸任的79岁的美联储主席艾伦·格林斯潘，如今终于尘埃落定：上周格林斯潘和伯南克大步走入总统办公室，接受布什总统宣布的任命。格林斯潘这位被称为"艺

---

[3] buff [bʌf] n.爱好者，迷；热心者
[4] grail [greil] n. 长期以来梦寐以求的东西
[5] wafer ['weifə] n. 薄脆饼

the man known as the Maestro will finally turn over his baton.[6]

Economists applauded the choice, the stock market rose, and even in partisan[7] Washington, it was hard to find anyone who disapproved. That's partly because of Bernanke's stellar[8] credentials[9], which drew immediate comparisons to the choice of John Roberts for the Supreme Court. In academic circles, Bernanke is regarded as a superstar; at the White House, he won favor by not talking down to the president, as economists sometimes do. Bernanke's other advantages: he's been confirmed by the Senate for three prior jobs and he's so moderate politically (or discreet[10]) that close colleagues claimed to have no idea whether he's a Democrat or, as it turned out, a Republican.

His study on the Great Depression is also great preparations for running a central bank. That's partly why, after long stints as a professor at Stanford and Princeton, he was tapped in 2002 by the Bush Administration to serve as one of seven Federal Reserve governors. There, as Greenspan furiously[11]

术大师"的老人在领导美联储长达18年后,终于将把权杖交给伯南克。

经济学家对这一选择表示了欢迎,股市应声上扬,即使在有着党派之见的华盛顿,也很难找到持反对意见的人士。这一方面归因于伯南克拥有出众的资历,人们一下子会把他与被选为最高法院首席大法官的约翰·罗伯茨作一比较。在学术界,伯南克被尊为超级明星。在白宫,他不会在总统面前用高人一等的口吻说话,因而受到青睐,而经济学家有时会犯这样的毛病。伯南克的其他优势包括:以前的三份工作已经得到了参议院的肯定;在政治立场上态度温和(或者说态度谨慎),就连亲密的同僚也声称不知道他到底是民主党派还是共和党派(其实他是共和党派)。

他对于经济大萧条的研究也为掌管中央银行做好了充分的准备。同时,从某种意义上讲,也算解释了为什么伯南克在斯坦福大学和普林斯顿大学长期任教后,会在2002年被布什政府选定为联邦储备委员会七名成员之一。就在网络经

---

6 baton ['bætən] *n.*官杖、权杖(某些国家用以表示官职、军衔等的短杖)

7 partisan [pɑːtiˈzæn] *a.*党徒的,党派性的

8 stellar ['stelə] *a.*主要的,显著的

9 credential [kriˈdenʃəl] *n.* [常用复]信任状、证书

10 discreet [disˈkriːt] *a.*(在行动、说话等方面)谨慎的,考虑周到的

11 furiously ['fjuəriəsli] *ad.* 强烈地

cut interest rates in the wake of the dot-com crash，Bernanke began speaking out about a different concern: deflation[12]. As the Fed moved short-term rates toward 1 percent—a historic low—Bernanke worried that if the economy slowed and prices began falling, the United States might encounter the stagnation[13] faced by Japan in the 1990s. "He's been treated somewhat unfairly by people who have accused him creating a deflation scare that was unwarranted," says Michael Prell, a former top Fed economist. Though the threat never materialized, Bernanke's boosters[14] say he was doing exactly what a Fed official should: scanning the horizon, assessing threats to the economy and devising pre-emptive solutions.

That doesn't mean he needs to give speeches about those risks, however. The deflation episode illustrates what may become a key distinction between Greenspan and his successor: while Greenspan obfuscated[15], Bernanke has a reputation for speaking clearly and espousing[16] openness. "Some academics find it hard to leave academia and talk more broadly, but Ben is so tremendously articulate[17]," says N. Gregory Mankiw, the

济崩溃后，格林斯潘执掌的美联储竭力下调利率的同时，伯南克开始就另一个问题——通货紧缩畅所欲言。随着美联储把短期利率调整至1%——创下了历史最低纪录，伯南克担心：如果经济增速减慢、物价开始下降，美国可能会像日本在20世纪90年代那样遭遇经济停滞。以前的美联储知名经济学家迈克尔·普莱尔说："伯南克多少遭到了一些人的不公正对待，有人指责他会引发不一定会发生的通货紧缩恐慌。"虽然通货紧缩威胁从来没有出现，但伯南克的支持者们说，他做到了美联储官员的本职工作：分析远景，评估国家经济所面临的威胁，并拿出先发制人的解决办法。

不过，这并不是说他需要就这些风险发表观点。对通货紧缩的不同态度也许表明了格林斯潘与其接班人的重要区别：格林斯潘含糊其辞，伯南克却以观点鲜明、直率坦诚而出名。"一些人士离开学术界后，很难进行更为广泛的谈论，但本却是极其善于表达，"哈佛大学的N.格里高利·曼昆教授说，他是伯南克前一任的布什政府首席经济顾问。除了演讲之外，伯南克还

---

[12] deflation [diˈfleiʃən] *n.* 通货紧缩
[13] stagnation[stægˈneiʃən] *n.*（经济）停滞
[14] booster [ˈbuːstə] *n.*支援者，支持者
[15] obfuscated [ˈɔbfʌskeitid] *a.* [美方] 被困惑住的，不知所措的
[16] espouse [isˈpauz] *vt.*拥护，信奉，支持；采纳
[17] articulate [ɑːˈtikjulit] *vi.*清楚地讲话

Harvard professor who preceded Bernanke as Bush's top economic adviser. Aside from speeches, Bernanke has supported other measures to make the Fed's workings less secretive, including a policy of "inflation targeting" that makes it clearer how much prices can rise before the Fed will raise rates to constrain them. Greenspan, a former jazz clarinetist[18], prefers a more flexible approach that allows for improvisation[19], as do other Fed officials. Most observers expect Bernanke to move cautiously in trying to implement such measures. Unlike Greenspan, he's also expected to avoid commenting on matters of broader policy—Social Security reform, tax cuts—for the foreseeable future.

When it comes to monetary policy, Fed watchers expect Bernanke to behave like Greenspan. By the time he takes his seat at the Fed's mammoth[20] mahogany[21] table in late March, the bank will have likely raised rates at 14 consecutive meetings. It's hard to say if the new Chairman will continue that tightening: the economy can change a lot in five months, as Katrina and America's recent brush with $ 3-a-gallon gas have reminded us. For now, despite rising energy costs, early signs of a softening housing

支持增强美联储工作透明度的其他措施，包括实行"盯住通货紧缩"政策，使得在美联储上调利率以控制物价之前物价会上涨多少变得更加明晰。曾在爵士乐队吹过单簧管的格林斯潘与美联储的其他官员一样，偏爱比较灵活的方法，那样就有即兴发挥的余地。大多数观察人士预计，伯南克在实施这些措施方面会比较谨慎。虽与格林斯潘不同，人们预计他也会避免对可以预见的将来的比较广泛的政策问题发表评论，譬如社会保障改革和减税等。

说到货币政策，美联储的观察人士预计伯南克的举措会与格林斯潘类似。等到3月底他在美联储那张偌大的红木办公桌旁边就座时，央行很可能会是已经连续第14次开会提高利率了。现在很难断定这位新主席是否会继续采用这种紧缩措施：5个月后经济会发生很大变化，正如卡特里娜飓风及美国最近油价飙升（已涨到每加仑3美元）提醒我们的那样。眼下，尽管能源成本不断上升，而且早早露出了房

---

[18] clarinetist [ˌklæri'netist] n. 单簧管手
[19] improvisation [ˌimprəvai'zeiʃən] n. 即席创作；即席演奏（或演唱）
[20] mammoth ['mæməθ] a. 巨大的，庞大的
[21] mahogany [mə'hɔɡəni] n. 红木，桃花心木

market and falling consumer confidence, talk of recession[22] remains negligible[23].

Before Bernanke can take command, however, Greenspan will take his final curtain call. If the Fed were a sports arena, his trademark dark suit would soon hang from the rafters[24]; this being Washington, his retirement will probably be marked instead by his own Fed party, where he'll take his chair home too. When the applause stops, Greenspan's legacy—presiding over the 1990s boom and responding deftly[25] to assorted[26] crises—will likely only grow larger. "I think Greenspan will go down in the history books as the greatest central banker up until this time," says MIT Nobel laureate Paul Samuelson. As his successor prepares to sit at his desk, we can only hope Greenspan has the good sense to pre-program his own home phone number into the speed dial.

地产市场趋于疲软和消费者信心趋于下跌的迹象，但经济衰退传闻仍显得无关紧要。

不过，在伯南克掌管大权之前，格林斯潘将进行最后的谢幕表演。如果说美联储是个运动场，那么他那标志性的黑色西服很快就会高高挂起；不过，这是在华盛顿，美联储会为格林斯潘举行欢送会，以此庆祝他的退休：到时格林斯潘也会把他的椅子带回家。等到曲终人散，格林斯潘的传奇色彩——领导美国实现20世纪90年代的经济繁荣、灵活应对各种各样的危机——可能只会越来越浓厚。麻省理工学院的诺贝尔奖获得者保罗·萨缪尔森说："我认为，作为迄今为止最伟大的央行行长，格林斯潘将会被载入史册。"就在他的接班人准备接过权杖之际，我们只希望格林斯潘有先见之明，事先把自己家的电话号码设成快速拨号键，以便伯南克可以随时向自己讨教。

---

[22] recession [ri'seʃən] *n.*（工商业的）衰退；（价格的）暴跌
[23] negligible ['neglidʒəbl] *a.*可以忽略的，微不足道的
[24] rafter ['rɑ:ftə] *n.*[建]椽
[25] deftly [deftli] *ad.* 灵巧地，熟练地
[26] assorted [ə'sɔ:tid] *a.*各式各样的，混杂的

财经宝库

1. 本文摘自《新闻周刊》（*Newsweek*），2005年11月7日。

2. Federal Reserve System美国联邦储备系统，简称Fed，负责履行美国中央银行的职责，这个系统是根据《联邦储备法案》于1913年成立的。它的主要职责有：① 制定并负责实施有关的货币政策；② 对银行机构实行监管，并保护消费者合法的信贷权利；③ 维持金融系统的稳定；④ 向美国政府、公众、金融机构和外国金融机构等提供可靠的金融服务。这个系统主要由联邦储备委员会、联邦储备银行及联邦公开市场委员会等组成。

3. Federal Reserve Board，简称美联储，它的全称叫 The Board of Governors of The Federal Reserve System，即联邦储备系统管理委员会，也可以称之为联邦储备系统理事会，它是一个联邦政府机构，其办公地点位于美国华盛顿特区（Washington D.C.）。该委员会由七名成员组成（其中主席和副主席各一位，委员五名），须由美国总统提名，经美国国会参议院批准方可上任，任期为十四年（主席和副主席任期为四年，可连任）。联邦储备委员会是联邦储备系统的核心机构。

4. Council of Economic Advisors，美国总统经济顾问委员会，它是美国总统办事机构的一部分，由一些经济学家组成并为美国总统提供相关咨询，它为白宫提供了大量的经济政策。该委员会共有20名资深经济学家，其中包括三名由总统提名再经参议院批准通过的委员。在这三人中，总统还将任命一人为委员会主席。

5. Alan Greenspan，艾伦·格林斯潘，1926年3月6日生于纽约市，1987年8月被里根总统任命为联邦储备委员会主席。1991年7月，布什总统任命格林斯潘继续担任联邦储备委员会主席。1996年2月，克林顿总统提名他连任联邦储备委员会主席，6月20日参议院以压倒多数批准了提名。2000年1月4日，克林顿总统再次任命他为美联储主席，同年6月20日，他第四次就任该职。

6. the Great Depression，经济大萧条，特指20世纪30年代使成百万美国人失业的一场世界范围内的经济危机。

7. the Civil War美国内战，1861年4月至1865年4月，美国

1932年，纽约，人们排队等待领取面包

南方与北方之间进行的战争，又称美国内战。北方领导战争的是资产阶级，战斗力量是广大工人、农民和黑人。在南方，坚持战争的只是种植园主，他们进行战争的目的是要把奴隶制度扩大到全国，北方目的则在于打败南方，以恢复全国统一。

8. deflation 通货紧缩，市场上流通的货币减少，人们的货币所得减少，购买力下降，影响物价之下跌，造成通货紧缩。长期的货币紧缩会抑制投资与生产，导致失业率升高及经济衰退。

DIY工作室

1. As Fed chairman，why Ben Bernanke's job was so important?

2. What are Ben's main economic views?

3. In which way is Ben Bernanke different from Alan Greenspan? Can you explain it in details?

归类记忆卡片

通货膨胀 inflation	双位数通货膨胀 double-digit inflation
宽松的财政政策 slack fiscal policy	恶性通货膨胀 hyperinflation
财政部 Treasury Department	长期通货膨胀 chronic inflation
增值税 VAT（value added tax）	治理通货膨胀 to fight inflation
赤字 deficit	货币控制工具 instruments of monetary control

复苏 recovery
生产率 productivity
资本市场 capital market
成本推进式通货膨胀 cost-push inflation
需求拉动式通货膨胀 demand-pull inflation

托收系统 collection system
资金划拨 transfer of funds
利润 profit
外汇储备 foreign exchange reserves
资本流动性 capital liquidity

听力广场

Ben Bernanke: the Federal Reserve is ready to cut interest rates aggressively

By AP with CNBC.com Jan.10, 2008

In a dramatic change of tone，Ben Bernanke yesterday indicated that the Federal Reserve is ready to cut interest rates aggressively to ward off the risk of a US recession.

The Fed chairman said "we stand ready to take substantive[27] additional action as needed to support growth and to provide additional insurance against downside risks".

The language—which initially sent stocks soaring—represents a new message from the Fed，which as recently as December emphasized

本·伯南克：美联储准备大力降息

美联储主席本·伯南克的口气出现明显变化，他昨日表示，美联储准备大力降息，以避免美国经济出现衰退的风险。

伯南克表示："我们已做好准备，在必要时采取大量附加行动，以支持经济增长，并提供额外保障，以防范下行风险。"

此番言论代表了来自美联储的最新讯息，就在去年12月份，美联储强调经济前景的不确定性。此言

---

[27] substantive [ˈsʌbstəntiv] a. 大量的，巨额的

the uncertainty surrounding the economic outlook.

Investors said Mr. Bernanke's comments would reinforce[28] expectations the Fed will cut interest rates by 50 basis points at its policy meeting this month.

The S&P 500 index, which had been down, rallied[29] sharply, though gains later subsided. Treasury yields pared their earlier rise, while the dollar fell against the euro, trading 0.8 percent lower at $1.4783.

The Fed chairman said demand for housing "seems to have weakened further". High oil prices, lower equity[30] prices and softening home values were also likely to "weigh on consumer spending".

He warned that the financial situation "remains fragile[31] and many funding markets remain impaired". Financial conditions "continue to pose a downside risk to the outlook for growth".

Earlier, the European Central Bank stepped up its warnings that eurozone rates may yet rise, even though the ECB left rates unchanged at 4 per cent.

Jean-Claude Trichet, ECB president, said

一出，股市起初应声飙升。

投资者表示，伯南克讲话将增强市场有关美联储将在本月的货币政策会议上降息50个基点的预期。

一直处于跌势的标准普尔500指数（S&P 500）大幅上涨，不过后来涨幅收窄。美国国债收益率回吐了早些时候的涨幅，美元兑欧元汇率下跌0.8%，至1欧元兑1.4783美元。

伯南克表示，住宅需求"似乎已进一步走软"。油价高企、股价下跌及房价不断缩水也可能"压制消费支出"。

他警告，金融形势"仍较为脆弱，许多资金市场仍未恢复"。金融状况"继续对经济增长前景形成一种下行风险"。

早些时候，欧洲央行（ECB）加大警告力度，称欧元区利率水平仍有可能上升，尽管欧洲央行将利率维持在4%不变。

欧洲央行行长让·克劳德·特

---

[28] reinforce [ˌriːinˈfɔːs] *v.*加强，增强
[29] rally [ˈræli] *v.*（股票市场等）价格止跌，回稳
[30] equity [ˈekwiti] *n.*（无固定利息的）股票、证券
[31] fragile [ˈfrædʒail] *a.*脆弱的，虚弱的

the bank was prepared to act "pre-emptively[32]" to avoid excessive wage demands.

But Mr. Trichet admitted that risks to the US economy were materializing[33] and announced two fresh auctions for US dollar liquidity[34] this month. Meanwhile, the Bank of England also left UK interest rates unchanged.

里谢（Jean-Claude Trichet）表示，欧洲央行准备"先发制人"，以避免过度的工资需求。

但特里谢承认，美国经济所面临的风险正不断成为现实，他本月宣布了两次新的美元流动性拍卖。与此同时，英国央行（Bank of England）也维持英国利率不变。

非常点拨

1. S&P 500 index，标准普尔500指数，该指数是记录美国500家上市公司的一个股票指数。这个股票指数由标准普尔公司创建并维护。标准普尔500指数覆盖的所有公司，都是在美国主要交易所，如纽约证券交易所、纳斯达克交易的上市公司。与道·琼斯指数相比，标准普尔500指数包含的公司更多，因此风险更为分散，能够反映更广泛的市场变化。

2. the European Central Bank，欧洲中央银行（ECB），是根据1992年《马斯特里赫特条约》的规定于1998年7月1日正式成立的，其前身是设在法兰克福的欧洲货币局。欧洲央行的职能是"维护货币的稳定"，管理主导利率、货币的储备和发行以及制定欧洲货币政策；其职责和结构以德国联邦银行为模式，独立于欧盟机构和各国政府之外。

欧洲中央银行是世界上第一个管理超国家货币的中央银行。独立性是它的一个显著特点，它不接受欧盟领导机构的指令，不受各国政府的监督。它是唯一有资格在欧盟内部发行欧元的机构，1999年1月1日欧元正式启动后，11个欧元区成员国政府将失去制定货币政策的权力，而必须实行欧洲中央银行制定的货币政策。

3. Eurozone，欧元区，是指欧盟成员中使用欧盟的统一货币——欧元的国家区域。由于英国、瑞典和丹麦决定暂不加入欧元区，目前，使用欧元的国家为德国、法国、意大利、荷兰、比利时、卢森堡、爱尔兰、希腊、西班牙、葡萄牙、奥地利、芬兰、斯洛文尼亚、塞浦路斯和马耳他。

---

[32] pre-emptively [pri(:)'emptivli] *ad.* （桥牌中的叫牌、进攻等）先发制人地
[33] materialize [mə'tiəriəlaiz] *v.* 成为事实
[34] liquidity [li'kwiditi] *n.* 流动性，流畅

19

Warren Buffett

Unit 2

Warren Buffett
世界投资大师：沃伦·巴菲特

主题札记

　　沃伦·巴菲特被喻为"当代最成功的投资者"。在历史上伟大的投资家中，巴菲特以他敏锐的业务评估技术引人注目。巴菲特是个纯粹的投资商，他从零开始，仅仅从事股票和企业投资，已成为当今世界大富豪之一。在40年的时间里，从艾森豪威尔时代到比尔·克林顿时期，无论股市行情牛气冲天抑或疲软低迷，无论经济繁荣抑或是不景气，巴菲特在市场上的表现总是非常好。巴菲特有丰富的人生经历和人格魅力，他简单质朴却又奥妙无穷的投资哲学和投资策略吸引着众多的投资者和企业管理决策者。他们每年一次像圣徒一样到奥马哈朝圣——聆听巴菲特的投资分析。这如同埃尔·沃斯音乐会或宗教复活节一样，成了美国每年一度的大事。金融界的人士把巴菲特的著作视为《圣经》，犹如念布道的经文一样背诵巴菲特的格言。

阅读长廊

The Master of Investment: Warren Buffett

For someone who is such an extraordinarily successful investor, Warren Buffett comes off as a pretty ordinary guy. Born and bred in Omaha, Nebraska, for more than 40 years Buffett has lived in the same gray stucco[1] house on Farnam Street that he bought for $31,500. He wears rumpled,[2] nondescript[3] suits, drives his own car, drinks Cherry Coke, and is more likely to be found in a Dairy Queen than a four-star restaurant.

But the 68-year-old Omaha native has led an extraordinary life. Looking back on his childhood, one can see the budding of a savvy[4] businessman. Warren Edward Buffett was born on August 30, 1930, the middle child of three. His father, Howard Buffett, came from a family

世界投资大师：沃伦·巴菲特

作为一个如此卓越的投资家，沃伦·巴菲特却又是一个非常平凡、普通的人。巴菲特在美国内布拉斯加州的奥马哈出生、长大，40多年来他一直居住的是法钠姆大街那栋自己以31,500美元购置的灰色水泥墙的房子。他穿皱巴巴的普通西装，亲自开车，常喝"樱桃可乐"，多数情况下是光顾"戴瑞王后"这样的小饭馆，而不是四星级的豪华酒店。

但这位68岁、土生土长的奥马哈人却有着不平凡的生活经历。回顾他的童年时代，就可以很好地了解这个机敏的生意人的成长过程。沃伦·爱德华·巴菲特生于1930年8月30日，在家里3个孩子中排行老二。他父亲霍华德·巴菲特成长于

---

[1] stucco ['stʌkəu] *n.* 拉毛水泥
[2] rumple ['rʌmpl] *vt. &vi.* 弄皱，压皱，弄乱
[3] nondescript ['nɔndis'kript] *a.* （因无特征而）难以归类的；难以形容的
[4] savvy ['sævi] *a.* 精明老练的，有见识的

of grocers but himself became a stockbroker[5] and later a US congressman[6].

Even as a young child, Buffett was pretty serious about making money. He used to go door-to-door and sell soda pop. He and a friend used math to develop a system for picking winners in horse racing and started selling their "Stable-Boy Selections" tip sheets until they were shut down for not having a license. Later, he also worked at his grandfather's grocery store. At the ripe age of 11, Buffett bought his first stock.

When his family moved to Washington D.C., Buffett became a paperboy for *The Washington Post* and its rival the *Times-Herald*. Buffett ran his five paper routes like an assembly line and even added magazines to round out his product offerings. While still in school, he was making $175 a month, a full-time wage for many young men.

When he was 14, Buffett spent $1,200 on 40 acres of farmland in Nebraska and soon began collecting rent from a tenant farmer. He and a friend also made $50 a week by placing pinball[7] machines in barber shops. They called their venture Wilson Coin Operated Machine

一个杂货商的家庭中，但后来却成了一名股票经纪人，之后又成为美国国会的议员。

甚至在很小的时候，巴菲特就对赚钱很用心。那时他常常挨家挨户地推销苏打汽水。他和一个朋友利用数学知识开发了一个在赛马比赛中选拔冠军的识别系统，然后开始推销他们的"马童筛选器"的内部消息传单，但因为无许可证被迫关停。后来，他还在祖父的杂货店干过一段时间。在11岁的时候，已近成熟的巴菲特买进了自己的第一只股票。

在巴菲特全家搬至华盛顿特区后，他开始为《华盛顿邮报》和该报的对手《时代先驱报》送报纸。巴菲特把自己送报的5条线路安排得就像生产线一样有条不紊，后来他甚至还添加了杂志的递送，这样他提供的订阅品种就更丰富了。在校读书期间，他每月的收入就已经有175美元了，相当于当时年轻人全职工作的月收入。

14岁那年，巴菲特花了1,200美元在内布拉斯加州购置了一片40公顷的农田，然后开始从佃户那里收取租金。他还和一个朋友为理发店安装弹球游戏机从而每周赚得50美元。他们把自己的"企业"称做"威尔森钱币运作机器公司"。

---

5 stockbroker ['stɔkbrəukə(r)] *n.* 代客买卖的证券经纪人
6 congressman ['kɔŋgresmən] *n.* 国会议员（尤指美国众议员）
7 pinball ['pinbɔːl] *n.* 弹球戏（一种用弹簧锤把弹子沿槽击至斜板顶部然后任其下滚落入各种规定部分而得分的游戏）pinball machine 弹球机

Company.

Already a successful albeit small—time businessman, Buffett wasn't keen on going to college but ended up at Wharton at the University of Pennsylvania—his father encouraged him to go. After two years at Wharton, Buffett transferred to his parents' alma mater[8], the University of Nebraska in Lincoln, for his final year of college. There Buffett took a job with the *Lincoln Journal* supervising 50 paperboys in six rural counties.

Buffett applied to Harvard Business School but was turned down in what had to be one of the worst admissions decisions in Harvard history. The outcome ended up profoundly[9] affecting Buffett's life, for he ended up attending Columbia Business School, where he studied under revered[10] mentor[11] Benjamin Graham, the father of securities analysis who provided the foundation for Buffett's investment strategy.

From the beginning, Buffett made his fortune from investing. He started with all the money he had made from selling pop, delivering papers, and operating pinball machines. Between 1950 and 1956, he grew his $9,800 kitty to $14,000. From there, he organized investment

这时巴菲特尽管并不起眼，但已是一个小获成功的商人。他对上大学并不感兴趣，不过后来还是在父亲的敦促下去了宾夕法尼亚大学的沃顿学院。在沃顿学习了两年后，巴菲特转学到其父母的母校——林肯的内布拉斯加大学，在那儿修完了大学最后一年的课程。期间巴菲特还在《林肯日报》谋得了一份工作，负责管理6个乡村地区的50个报童。

巴菲特曾申请哈佛商学院，但是被拒绝，这后来成为哈佛历史上最糟糕的录取决定之一。这个结果对巴菲特的一生产生了深远的影响，他因此进入哥伦比亚商学院，并师从著名的证券分析之父本杰明·格雷厄姆，巴菲特从证券分析之父身上学到的东西为日后形成自己的投资策略奠定了基础。

一开始，巴菲特凭借投资来赚钱。他最初的资本来自卖苏打汽水、送报纸和安装弹球游戏机而攒下的积蓄。在1950年到1956年，他的积蓄由9,800美元升至14,000美元。此后，巴菲特开始与家人和朋友结成伙伴投资关系，后来又凭借

---

[8] alma mater ['ælmə 'meitə] *n.* [拉]母校
[9] profoundly [prə'faundli] *ad.*深深地，深切地
[10] rever [ri'viə] *v.* 尊敬，崇敬，敬畏
[11] mentor ['mentɔ:] *n.* 良师益友，导师

partnerships with his family and friends, and then gradually drew in other investors through word of mouth and very attractive terms.

Buffett's goal was to top the Dow Jones Industrial Average by an average of 10% a year. Over the length of the Buffett partnership between 1957 and 1969, Buffett's investments grew at a compound annual rate of 29.5%, crushing[12] the Dow's return of 7.4% over the same period.

Buffett's investment strategy mirrors his lifestyle and overall philosophy. He doesn't collect houses or cars or works of art, and he disdains[13] companies that waste money on such extravagances[14] as limousines[15], private dining rooms, and high-priced real estate. He is a creature of habit—same house, same office, same city, same soda—and dislikes change. In his investments, that means holding on to "core holdings" such as American Express, Coca-Cola, and The Washington Post Co. "forever".

Buffett's view of inherited money also departs from the norm. Critical of the self-indulgence[16] of the super-rich, Buffett thinks

口头游说和一些优惠条件拉拢其他投资者。

巴菲特的目标是以每年平均10%的比率超出道·琼斯工业指数。在巴菲特倡导的"合伙投资"模式下，从1957年到1969年，巴菲特的投资以每年29.5%的综合速度增长，大大超过了道·琼斯在同一时期7.4%的回报率。

巴菲特的投资策略可映射出他的生活方式和人生哲学。他没有囤积房屋、收集汽车和艺术品的嗜好，他厌恶那些把钱花在高级轿车、私人餐厅和豪华地产这类奢侈品上的公司。他是个善于遵循习惯的人——住同一栋房屋，在同一间办公室办公，在同一个城市生活，喝同一牌子的可乐，他不喜欢变化。用在他的投资理念上，就是紧抓住投资"核心"不变，如美国捷运公司、可口可乐、华盛顿邮报公司，而且是"永远不变"。

巴菲特对待遗产的态度也与众不同。他对"超级富人"自我放纵的生活方式非常反感，他把遗产

---

[12] crush [krʌʃ] vt. 压服，压倒，压垮
[13] disdain[dis'dein] vt. 轻视，鄙视
[14] extravagance [iks'trævəgəns] n.奢侈，铺张，浪费
[15] limousine ['limu(:)zi:n] n. 轿车，（前后座用玻璃隔开的）大型高级轿车
[16] indulgence [in'dʌldʒəns] n.任性，放肆，沉溺，着迷

of inheritances[17] as "privately funded food stamps" that keep children of the rich from leading normal, independent lives. With his own three kids, he gave them each $10,000 a year—the tax—deductible[18] limit—at Christmas. When he gave them a loan, they had to sign a written agreement. When his daughter, also named Susie like her mother, needed $20 to park at the airport, he made her write him a check for it.

As for charity, Buffett's strict standards have made it difficult for him to give much away. He evaluates charities the same way he looks for stocks: value for money, return on invested capital. He has established the Buffett Foundation, designed to accumulate[19] money and give it away after his and his wife's deaths—though the foundation has given millions to organizations involved with population control, family planning, abortion[20], and birth control. The argument goes that Buffett can actually give away a greater sum in the end by growing his money while he's still alive.

One thing's for sure about Buffett: He's happy doing what he's doing. "I get to do what I like to do every single day of the year," he says.

看做是"私人资助的饭票"，这让有钱人家的孩子们无法过上正常而独立的生活。对自己的3个孩子，巴菲特在每年圣诞节时给他们每人1万美元作为一年的花销——免征所得税收的最低限度。若是给他们贷款，则需签订书面协议。有一次他的女儿苏茜——与母亲同名——在机场需要20美元的停车费，巴菲特虽然把钱借给了她，但却要求女儿给自己写了一张支票。

巴菲特严格的处事标准使他即使是面对慈善事业也很难慷慨解囊。他对待慈善事业的态度犹如对待股票：认真评估投入资本的有价回报。他成立了巴菲特基金会，意在积累资金，在自己和妻子死后发放。不过巴菲特基金会至今已为许多组织捐款数百万美元，资助的项目包括人口控制、计划生育、堕胎和避孕等。许多人认为通过进一步扩张现有财力，巴菲特在有生之年就可最终捐出一大笔款项。

对于巴菲特来说，有一点可以肯定：他非常热爱自己的工作。"一年中的每一天我都在做自己喜

---

[17] inheritance [in'heritəns] *n.* 遗产，继承物
[18] deductible [di'dʌktəbl] *a.* 可扣除的，可减免的
[19] accumulate [ə'kju:mjuleit] *vt.* 积累，积聚
[20] abortion [ə'bɔ:ʃən] *n.* 流产，小产，早产

"I get to do it with people I like, and I don't have to associate with anybody who causes my stomach to churn[21]. I tap dance to work, and when I get there I think I'm supposed to lie on my back and paint the ceiling. It's tremendous[22] fun." It's fun to watch the master at work, too.

欢做的事，我与自己喜欢的人一起工作。我用不着与自己讨厌的人打交道。我每天都跳着踢踏舞去工作，到了公司我会觉得工作就好像是让自己仰面躺下，用手中的笔绘制天花板一般轻松。工作让我乐趣无穷。"巴菲特说。当然，看一位大师级人物工作同样也是乐趣无穷。

财经宝库

　　1. Omaha，奥马哈，是美国内布拉斯加州（Nebraska）最大的城市。该城位于内布拉斯加州东部密苏里河畔。

　　2. Pennsylvania, 宾夕法尼亚州，是美国东部的一个州，为美国立国13州之一。该州自从建立之初就以宗教自由和政治民主著称，在北美有很大影响。美国历史上的许多重要篇章都是在宾夕法尼亚州谱写的，如《独立宣言》。州内最大的两个城市也是美国的大城市，是费城和匹兹堡，费城是美国独立战争时起草《独立宣言》和联邦宪法的地方，所以宾夕法尼亚州也被称为"美国的摇篮"，匹兹堡曾经是著名的钢铁城。

　　3. Benjamin Graham, 本杰明·格雷厄姆。股市向来被人视为精英聚集之地，华尔街则是衡量一个人智慧与胆识的决定性场所。本杰明·格雷厄姆作为一代宗师，他的金融分析学说和思想在投资领域产生了极为巨大的震动，影响了几乎三代重要的投资者，如今活跃在华尔街的数十位资产上亿的投资管理人都自称为格雷厄姆的信徒，他享有"华尔街教父"的美誉。

---

[21] churn [tʃə:n] *vi.* 剧烈搅动；（液体）打旋起泡；来回拍打；翻腾
[22] tremendous [tri'mendəs] *a.* 极大的，非常的，惊人的

4. *The Washington Post*，《华盛顿邮报》，该报是美国华盛顿哥伦比亚特区最大、历史最悠久的报纸。20世纪70年代初通过揭露水门事件——迫使理查德·尼克松总统退职，《华盛顿邮报》获得了国际威望。许多人认为它是继《纽约时报》后美国最有声望的报纸。由于位于美国首都，它尤其擅长报道美国国内政治动态，而《纽约时报》则在报道国际事务上更加有威望。也有人指责《华盛顿邮报》过分关心政治而忽略了对其他方面的报道。

华盛顿邮报

5. 巴菲特的经典语录

"一生能够积累多少财富，不取决于你能够赚多少钱，而取决于你如何投资理财，钱找人胜过人找钱，要懂得让钱为你工作，而不是你为钱工作。"

"我从11岁开始就在做资金分配这个工作，一直到现在都是如此。"

"就算美联储主席格林斯潘偷偷告诉我他未来两年的货币政策，我也不会改变我的任何一项行动。"

"从预言中你可以得知许多预言者的信息，但对未来却所获无几。"

"我有一个内部得分牌。如果我做了某些其他人不喜欢，但我感觉良好的事，我会很高兴。如果其他人称赞我所做过的事，但我自己却不满意，我不会高兴的。"

"如果市场总是有效的，我只会成为一个在大街上手拎马口铁罐的流浪汉。"

"在一个人们相信市场有效性的市场里投资，就像与某个被告知看牌没有好处的人在一起打桥牌。"

"目前的金融课程可能只会帮助你作出庸凡之事。"

"没有一个能计算出内在价值的公式。你得懂这个企业（你得懂得打算购买的这家企业的业务）。"

"不必等到企业降至谷底才去购买它的股票。所选企业股票的售价要低于你所认为的它的价值并且企业要由诚实而有能力的人经营。但是，你若能以低于一家企业目前价值的钱买进它的股份，你对它的管理有信心，同时你又买进了一批类似于该企业的股份，那你赚钱就指日可待了。"

"今天的投资者不是从昨天的增长中获利的。"

DIY工作室

1. What kind of life does the successful investor—Warren Buffett like to live?
2. Can you explain some points of Buffett's investment strategy?

归类记忆卡片

利润 profit
投资回报 return on investment
补偿贸易 compensatory trade, compensated
单一的实体 a single entity
抵押贷款 mortgage lending
业主产权 owner's equity
普通股 common stock
无形资产 intangible assets
机构投资者 institutional investor
投资银行 investment bank

代销 offer for sale
定向发行 introduction
直销 placing
公开发行 public issue
信贷额度 credit line
国际债券 international bonds
利差 interest margin
权利股发行 rights issue
净收入比例结合 net income gearing
损益表 income statement

听力广场

The Definition of Happiness

Emory:

How do you define happiness and what about your life makes you most happy? When you make good on an investment, do you allow yourself to enjoy that success by getting excited- and on the flip-side, when an investment turns down, do you find yourself equally disappointed—or do you try to remove emotion from your work, as much as possible?

Buffett:

I enjoy what I do, I tap dance to work every day. I work with people I love, doing what I love. The only thing I would pay to get rid of is firing people. I spend my time thinking about the future, not the past. The future is exciting. As Bertrand Russell says, "Success is getting what you want, happiness is wanting what you get." I won the ovarian[23] lottery the day I was born and so did all of you. We're all

幸福的定义

Emory大学学生：

你怎么定义幸福？你生活中的什么事使你感觉最幸福？当你做了一笔成功的投资时，你会允许自己兴高采烈地享受成功吗？从另一面讲，如果一笔投资失败了，你会不会感觉到同样的失望？或者，你会试图尽一切可能不让感情因素影响你的工作？

巴菲特：

我享受我做的事情，我每天都跳着踢踏舞去工作。我和我喜欢的人一起工作，做我喜欢的事情。我唯一希望尽可能避免的事情是解雇员工。我把我的时间用来思考未来，而不是过去。未来是激动人心的。正如伯特兰·罗素说

伯特兰·罗素

---

[23] ovarian [əuˈvɛəriən] a. [解] 卵巢的

successful, intelligent, educated. To focus on what you don't have is a terrible mistake. With the gifts all of us have, if you are unhappy, it's your own fault.

I know a woman in her 80's, a Polish Jew woman forced into a concentration camp with her family but not all of them came out. She says, "I am slow to make friends because when I look at people, I have one question in mind; would they hide me?" If you get to be my age, or younger for that matter, and have a lot of people that would hide you, then you can feel pretty good about how you've lived your life. I know people on the Forbes 400 list whose children would not hide them. "He's in the attic, he's in the attic." Some of them keep compensating by joining board seats or getting honorary degrees, but it doesn't change the fact that no one will give a damn[24] when they are gone. The most powerful force in the world is unconditional love. To horde it is a terrible mistake in life. The more you try to give it away, the more you get it back. At an individual level, it's important to make sure that for the people that count[25] to you, you count to them.

的，"成功是得到自己想要的，幸福是想要自己得到的"。我出生的那天赢得了卵巢彩票（注：指精子发育为受精卵的过程），你们所有人都一样。我们都很成功、聪明、受过教育。专注于那些你没有的东西是一个可怕的错误。有了我们人人拥有的天赋，如果你仍然不快乐，那是你自己的错误。

我认识一个80多岁的妇人，她是一个波兰犹太人，曾经和全家一起被赶进集中营，其中有人死在了里面。她说："我交朋友往往很慢，因为当我看着人们时，脑海中有一个问题：他们会把我藏起来吗？"如果你到了我这个岁数（注：沃伦·巴菲特已经年满77岁），或者年轻一点，而有一大群人愿意把你藏起来，那么你完全可以为自己过去的生活感到骄傲。我认识一些出现在福布斯400强富豪排行榜上的人，可他们的子女都不会把他们藏起来的。他们的子女会说："他在阁楼上面！他在阁楼上面！"其中有些人占据着董事会席位，或者获得名誉学位，借此补偿自己；但这不会改变这样的事实——在他们死了之后，没有人会有一丁点在乎他们。世界上最强大的力量是无条件的爱。把它私藏起来是人生的巨大错误。你给别人的爱越多，你获得的回报就越多。从

---

[24] damn [dæm] n. 丝毫
[25] count [kaunt] vi. 有价值，有重要意义，有影响

个人角度来讲，重要的是确保那些依靠你的人，你同样也可以依靠他们。

　　如果你能购买一个同班同学未来收入的10%，你会怎么做？你不会购买那些IQ最高或者成绩最好的人的收入，但你会买那些最实在的人的收入。你喜欢那些慷慨的人，尽力而为的人，正直坦率的人。现在想象一下你可以卖空你的一个同班同学的10%。这一般会更有趣，当你开始环顾整个房间的时候，你不会选择那些成绩最差的人。你会寻找那些没有人愿意与之相处的人，那些惹人厌恶或者只顾自己利益的人。如果你有一副500马力的引擎却只发挥出了50马力，你会被另外一个拥有300马力引擎却发挥出了250马力的人击败。潜在能力和实际发挥之间的区别取决于人的品质。你可以列出你最仰慕的品质，以及你最鄙视的品质。换一下角度，试想如果这是我对所列品质的反应，那么这个世界对我会有怎样的反应？你可以学着养成那些你想要的品质，摒弃那些你不想要的品质。习惯是很容易养成的，你不知不觉间就会被习惯束缚，等你察觉到了，又很难破坏它。你不可能

What if you could buy 10% of one of your classmates and their future earnings? You wouldn't buy the ones with the highest IQ, the best grades, etc., but the most effective[26]. You like people who are generous, go out of their way, straight shooters[27]. Now imagine that you could short[28] 10% of one of your classmates. This part is usually more fun as you start looking around the room. You wouldn't choose the ones with the poorest grades. Look for people nobody wants to be around, that are obnoxious[29] or like to take all the credit. If you have a 500 HP engine and only get 50 HP out of it, you'll be beaten by someone else that has a 300 HP engine but gets 250 HP output. The difference between potential and output comes from human qualities. You can make a list of the qualities you admire and those you despise[30]. To turn the tables[31], think if this is the way I react to the qualities on the list, which is the way the world will react to me. You can learn to turn on those qualities you want and turn off those qualities you wish to avoid. The chains of habit

---

[26] effective [i'fektiv] *a.* 实在的，实际的
[27] shooter ['ʃuːtə(r)] *n.* 射手，射击运动员
[28] short [ʃɔːt] *vi.* 卖空证券（或商品等）
[29] obnoxious [əb'nɔkʃəs] *a.* 令人非常不快的，引起反感的，讨厌的
[30] despise [dis'paiz] *vt.* 鄙视，藐视，看不起
[31] turn the table（s），转变形势，扭转局面，转败为胜

are too light to be felt until they are too heavy to be broken. You can't change at 60; the time to look at that list is now.

到了60岁才去改变，现在是该列一张单子的时候了。

非常点拨

1. Bertrand Russell，伯特兰·罗素（1872—1970），英国哲学家、数学家、社会学家，也是20世纪西方最著名、影响最大的学者和社会活动家。

2. the Forbes 400 list，福布斯400强。福布斯主要有三个含义。福布斯首先是个集团；其次是个人，全名是史提夫·福布斯，他是福布斯集团的总裁；最后是福布斯先生经营的世界上最著名的财经杂志《福布斯》。《福布斯》杂志是美国最早的大型商业杂志，它前瞻性强，有不妥协的精神，观点鲜明、不拘一格、简明扼要。较为著名的是福布斯富豪榜，这是全球最权威的财富排行榜。

Alan Greenspan
Unit 3

Alan Greenspan
美联储前主席：艾伦·格林斯潘

主题札记

有这么一个老头儿，他永远穿着深色西服，戴着黑框眼镜，白色的衬衣上配着一条不入时的细结领带，头发已经稀疏，一脸的褶子，说话前言不搭后语，总是一脸的沮丧。

就是这样一个人，却立于世界经济舞台的最前端，吸引了异乎寻常的注意力。自1987年出任美联储主席以来，他能够对经济形势进行冷静判断，并能果断采取有效措施，多次缓解危机，也赢得了人们的信任……

阅读长廊

Greenspan is Almost Hopeless

Alan Greenspan is an American economist and was from 1987 to 2006 the Chairman of the Federal Reserve of the United States.

Greenspan was born in 1926 to a Hungarian Jewish family in the Washington Heights area of New York City. He is an accomplished saxophone player who played with Stan Getz. While in college, he played in a jazz band. He then attended New York University （NYU）, and received a B.A. in economics in 1948, and a M.A. in economics in 1950. Greenspan went on to Columbia University, intending to pursue advanced economic studies, but subsequently dropped out.

Alan Greenspan has been married twice. His first marriage was to Joan Mitchell in 1952; the marriage ended in divorce one year later. He dated newswoman Barbara Walters in the late 1970s. In 1984, Greenspan began

格林斯潘
要无计可施了

艾伦·格林斯潘是美国经济学家，从1987年到2006年任美国联邦储备委员会主席。

1926年，格林斯潘出生于纽约城华盛顿海茨地区的一个匈牙利裔的犹太家庭。他是个娴熟的萨克斯管演奏家，和斯坦·歌茨一起演奏。在大学时代，他曾在一个爵士乐队演奏。他之后考上纽约大学，1948年获得经济学学士学位，1950年获得经济学硕士学位。学成之后，格林斯潘又去哥伦比亚大学，想继续经济领域的学习，但是后来放弃了。

艾伦·格林斯潘结过两次婚。他的第一次婚姻是1952年娶了琼·米歇尔，但是一年后就离婚了。在20世纪70年代，他与女新闻记者芭芭拉·华特斯约会。1984年，格林斯潘开始和记者安德里

dating journalist Andrea Mitchell. Greenspan at the time was 58, and the also once divorced Mitchell was 20 years his junior at the age of 38. In 1997, they were married by Supreme Court Justice Ruth Bader Ginsburg.

On May 18, 2004, Greenspan was nominated by President George W. Bush to serve for an unprecedented fifth term as chairman of the Federal Reserve. He was previously appointed to the post by Presidents Ronald Reagan, George H. W. Bush and Bill Clinton. Greenspan was awarded the Presidential Medal of Freedom, the highest civilian award in the United States, by President George W. Bush in November 2005.

Greenspan's term as a member of the Board ended on January 31, 2006, and Ben Bernanke was confirmed as his successor. Bernanke is a former chairman of the US President's Council of Economic Advisers, and his appointment is seen in part as a move to effect a smooth transition.

He has written his memoir, titled *The Age of Turbulence: Adventures in a New World,* published September 17, 2007. Greenspan says that he wrote this book in longhand mostly while soaking in the bathtub, a habit he regularly employs ever since an accident in 1971, when he injured his back. Greenspan discusses in his book, among other things, his history in government and economics, capitalism and

亚·米歇尔约会。当时格林斯潘58岁时，米歇尔比他小20岁，38岁，也离过婚。1997年，他们俩在最高法院法官鲁思·柏德尔·金斯博格的主持下举行了婚礼。

2004年5月18日，格林斯潘被乔治·布什总统任命为美联储主席，这是他第五次担任这个职位，这是史无前例的。之前他曾经被里根总统、老布什总统、克林顿总统等任命该职。格林斯潘于2005年11月被乔治·布什总统授予总统自由奖章，这是美国最高荣誉的文职奖章。

格林斯潘作为联邦储备委员会成员的职务于2006年1月31日到期，本·伯南克被确认是他的继任者。伯南克是美国总统经济顾问委员会的前任主席，他的任命从某种程度上讲，会实现平稳过渡。

格林斯潘写了回忆录——《动荡年代：新世界的冒险》，于2007年9月17日出版。格林斯潘说，他这本书大部分是他在浴缸里泡澡的时候亲手写的。自从他1971年因为一场事故背部受伤以后，他就养成了泡澡的习惯。在他的书里，除了其他一些事情，他还讲述了他在政府和经济领域的历史、资本主义和其他的经济模式、全球化经济中的

other modes of economies, current issues in the global economy, and future issues that face the global economy.

The US Federal Reserve has offered such an extraordinary stimulus[1] to the US economy for the past three years that America's official real interest rates are still in the remarkable state of being deeply negative. In June, Alan Greenspan, the Fed Chairman, and his colleagues started the long process of bringing rates back to a more normal level. But Friday's empolyment data must have given them a serious jolt[2].

It was just over five weeks ago that the Fed gingerly[3] edged up the main policy rate, the Fed funds rate, from its 46-year low of 1 percent to 1.25 percent. A neutral level— at which the economy is being neither stimulated nor restrained—should be about 4 percent for the US, according to economists at the Organization for Economic Co-operation and Development. Markets had been anticipating that the Fed would take the rate up to 2 percent by the end of the year. But the empolyment data were so feeble[4] that they stirred a storm of doubt. While the Wall Street had expected that about 215,000 new jobs would have been created in July, the

当前问题以及将要面临的问题。

过去的三年，美联储对美国经济给予了如此不同寻常的刺激，以致美国官方的实际利率至今仍然处于极低的负值水平。6月份，美联储主席艾伦·格林斯潘与他的同僚开始了一个长期的进程，要把利率调回到更为正常的水平。但上周五的就业数据一定使他们震惊。

仅在五周前，美联储谨慎地把主要政策利率——美国联邦基金利率小幅上调，从1%这个46年最低点调升至1.25%。经济合作与发展组织（OECD）经济学家说，对于美国来说，中等水平（经济既不受刺激，也不受抑制）应该为4%左右。市场曾一直预期，在年底美联储会把利率调升至2%。但是就业数据如此虚弱以致引起人们普遍的怀疑。华尔街曾预期7月份会创造大约21.5万个新的就业机会，而劳工部报告此数字仅为区区的3.2万。这已经是第二个月发布令人担心的薄弱数字了。关键问题是美国的经济复苏能否承受接近正常利率

---

[1] stimulus ['stimjuləs] *n.*刺激，刺激物，促进因素
[2] jolt [dʒəult] *n.* [喻]震惊，引起震惊的事情
[3] gingerly['dʒindʒəli] *ad.*小心谨慎地，战战兢兢地
[4] feeble ['fi:bl] *a.* 微弱的，薄弱的

Department of Labor reported that the number was a scant 32,000. It was the second month of worryingly weak numbers. The crucial question is whether America's economic recovery can bear the strain of anything even approaching a normal interest rate.

The Federal Open Market Committee, when it meets today, is expected to press ahead and raise the Fed funds rate once again by the same cautious increment[5] of 0.25 percentage points, taking the rate to 1.5 percent, But futures markets have shifted to reflect a new view on the chances that the Fed will continue its campaign into September; the odds have shifted from a 70 percent likelihood to only half that.

The FOMC members will have much to ponder. The market movements on Friday spotlight the twin dangers through which Mr. Greenspan must navigate the economy. The Dow Jones index of share prices fell by 1.5 percentage points to its lowest level for the year. Stock investors are anxious that the recovery is slowing unexpectedly. That is the first danger Mr. Greenspan must avoid.

But consider two other prices: the price of gold leapt by $7 an ounce to $402 after the report, and the price of oil remained at about $44

水平所带来的压力。

联邦公开市场委员会（FOMC）今天要举行会议，人们希望他们能顶住压力，再次谨慎地把联邦基金利率上调0.25个百分点，升至1.5%。但是期货市场改变了以往的观点，对联邦政府会继续加息到9月份的可能性反映出了自己的新观点，市场认为这种可能性已经从原来的70%降低到它的一半。

FOMC成员有许多需要仔细考虑的事情。上周五的市场走势暴露了格林斯潘所掌舵的经济一定会面临的双重危险。道·琼斯股票价格指数下跌了1.5个百分点，达到年度最低点。股票投资者很担心这种复苏正在出乎意料地减缓。这是格林斯潘先生必须避免的第一个危险。

但是考虑一下另外两个价格：在此报告出台后，黄金价格每盎司上涨了7美元，达到402美元；石

---

[5] increment ['inkrimənt] *n.* 增长，增额，增值

a barrel. These numbers suggest no slackening[6] in inflationary[7] pressures. If anything, they imply that inflation is returning. This is the second danger. Of course, the Fed's cure for inflation is to raise interest rates. Yet, with the recovery in an apparently delicate state, that could precipitate[8] a sharp slowing.

In all likelihood, the jobs figures will prove not to be a harbinger[9] of slump but an aberration[10], or handmaiden to a modest slowing in growth. There are too many signs of persistent recovery to believe that a crunch is upon us. From other July reports we know that motor vehicle sales were up strongly and retail sales in reasonable shape. Still, the troubling news is an important reminder of the restraints on US monetary policy, If anything were to go seriously wrong with the economy, the Fed would be more constrained in its options than it had been for many years. With official interest rates so low, there is very little scope for any meaningful cuts.

How did America get to this point? In 1996, Mr. Greenspan hovered in the brink of trying to manage the Wall Street bubble—remember his

油价格仍维持在每桶大约44美元。这些数字没有显示通货膨胀压力的减轻，却意味着通货膨胀正卷土重来。这是第二个风险。当然，美联储应对通货膨胀的措施是提高利率。然而，由于经济复苏显然处于一种脆弱状态，提高利率可能促成经济增长速度的急速下降。

在所有的可能性中，就业数字证明这不是经济衰退的先兆，而是一种暂时的波动现象，或是促成经济增长适度减缓的因素。众多的经济持续复苏的迹象使我们无法相信我们正面临被压垮的风险。从7月份的其他报告我们了解到，摩托车销售量增长强劲，零售业形势也不错。而且，这些令人困扰的消息提醒人们美国货币政策所面临的各种束缚。如果美国经济出了什么大问题的话，美联储会采取比过去多年更保守的举措。官方的利率如此低，几乎再没有任何有意义的减息空间。

美国是如何走到这一步的呢？1996年，格林斯潘先生曾就是否要治理华尔街的泡沫而思前想后——

---

[6] slacken ['slækən] v.（风等）减弱，变缓慢
[7] inflationary [in'fleiʃənəri] a. 通货膨胀的，由通货膨胀引起的
[8] precipitate [pri'sipiteit] v. 使突然发生；加速；促使
[9] harbinger ['hɑ:bindʒə] n. 预兆
[10] aberration [,æbə'reiʃn] n.离开正路，脱离常轨，过失

famous warning of "irrational[11] exuberance"[12]? But he decided that this was too politically risky. He instead accommodated the bubble, cheered on the so-called New Economy and waited for the bubble to burst.

In the following three years, the bubble bloated to become, in proportion to the US economy, more than twice the size of the one that had preceded the Great Crash of 1929. When it burst, Mr. Greenspan had to take extraordinary measures. His recovery plan took rates so low for so long that America's conventional monetary policy options now approach the point of exhaustion[13]. The problem Mr. Greenspan is trying to solve is one of his own making.

The other arms of US economic policy are constrained too. Fiscal policy is not in a robust condition to offer help. The Federal Budget is on course to be in deficit this year by $478bn—or 4.2 percent of gross domestic product—according to the Congressional Budget Office, and both George W. Bush and John Kerry, his Democratic challenger for the presidency, have pledged to halve the deficit over the next four years.

想必还记得他的著名的 "非理性繁荣" 的警告吧？但是他认为这在政治上太冒险了。相反，他姑息了这些泡沫，还为所谓的新经济喝彩，并等泡沫破裂。

在随后的三年中，泡沫在美国经济中的比例越来越大，达到1929年大萧条之前的泡沫的两倍多。一旦此泡沫破裂，格林斯潘先生将不得不采取非同寻常的举措。他的复苏计划使利率长期保持低水平，导致目前美国传统货币政策所能采取的措施接近枯竭。格林斯潘先生正在努力解决的问题正是他自己一手造成的。

美国经济政策的其他手段也受到限制。财政政策没有活力而无法提供帮助。美国国会预算办公室统计，联邦预算今年将出现4,780亿美元赤字——相当于国内生产总值的4.2％。乔治·沃克·布什和民主党总统竞选挑战者约翰·克里都已许诺，要在接下来的四年中使赤字减半。

---

[11] irrational [i'ræʃənəl] *a.*无理性的，不合理性的
[12] exuberance [ig'zju:bərəns] *n.*繁荣，充溢，丰富
[13] exhaustion [ig'zɔ:stʃən] *n.*耗尽，枯竭

There is some scope for using a cheaper dollar as a source of stimulus. It has fallen by 15 percent against main currencies in the past two years and it could fall further without serious consequences, although any precipitate plunge[14] could begin a rout. In sum, however, America already has pushed all three of its levers of macroeconomic stimulus fairly hard over to the "go" position. Mr. Greenspan must be praying that nothing goes awry in the year ahead.

把廉价美元作为经济刺激的原动力是可行的。在过去两年中，美元兑主要货币下跌了15%，还可能在不造成严重后果的情况下继续下跌，尽管美元的任何突如其来的下跌可能会导致美国经济的大崩溃。然而，总的来说，美国已经相当努力地推动了全部三个宏观经济刺激的杠杆，使其达到了"运转"的位置。格林斯潘先生一定在祈求来年一切顺利。

财经宝库

1. the Presidential Medal of Freedom，总统自由奖章，是美国最高荣誉的文职奖章，于1945年由杜鲁门政府首次颁发，当时是为了奖赏第二次世界大战中的功臣。

2. The Organization for Economic Co-operation and Development，经济合作与发展组织，简称经合组织（OECD），是由30个市场经济国家组成的政府间国际经济组织，旨在共同应对全球化带来的经济、社会和政府治理等方面的挑战，并把握全球化带来的机遇。经合组织的历史可以追溯到第二次世界大战后重建欧洲经济的马歇尔计划，其最初的宗旨一直延续到今天：促进成员国的持续经济增长、就业以及生活水平的提高，同时保持财政政策的稳定，以此对世界经济的发展作出贡献；帮助成员国和其他国家在经济发展进程中保持健康的经济增长步伐；在多边、平等的基础上促进世界贸易的繁荣。

---

[14] plunge [plʌndʒ] *n.*落下，下跌

3. The Federal Open Market Committee，联邦公开市场委员会，简称FOMC，它隶属于联邦储备系统，主要任务是确定美国货币政策，通过货币政策的调控达到经济成长及物价稳定两者间的平衡。FOMC制定的货币政策主要由纽约联邦储备银行来执行，而所谓的公开市场操作，通常是指调整联邦基金利率。

1. The Fed's cure for inflation is to raise interest rates. Do you think this is a good idea?

2. Whether America's economic recovery can bear the strain of anything even approaching a normal interest rate?

合同 contract	税法 tax bill
汇率 exchange rate	公共财政 public finance
紧缩信贷 tighten credit	财政部 Treasury Department
私营部门 private sector	平衡预算 balanced budget
财政当局 fiscal authorities	继承税 inheritance tax
宽松的财政政策 slack fiscal policy	复苏 recovery

增值税 VAT（value-added tax）　　　　赤字 deficit
收入 revenue　　　　　　　　　　　　萧条 recession
总需求 aggregate demand　　　　　　　经济好转 turnabout
货币化 monetization

听力广场

Alan Greenspan: House prices in the US are likely to fall significantly
（Sep.17,2007）

House prices in the US are likely to fall significantly from their present levels, Alan Greenspan has told *The Financial Times*, admitting for the first time that there was a bubble in the US housing market.

In an interview ahead of the release today of his memoirs, the former chairman of the Federal Reserve said the decline in house prices "is going to be larger than most people expect".

But Mr. Greenspan said that his successors at the Fed—who meet tomorrow to set interest rates—would have to be careful not to ease rates too aggressively, because the risk of an

2007年9月17日　格林斯潘警告：美国房价可能大幅下跌

美联储前主席艾伦·格林斯潘日前在接受英国《金融时报》采访时表示，美国房价可能较现有水平大幅下跌，这是他首次承认美国房地产市场存在泡沫。

今天，在他的回忆录发行仪式前接受采访时，格林斯潘称，房价的跌幅将"超出多数人的预期"。

但格林斯潘表示，他的那些继任者们（明天他们将开会确定利率）必须格外小心，降息幅度不要过大，因为目前"通胀抬头"的风

"inflationary resurgence[15]" was greater now than when he was Fed chief.

Mr. Greenspan said he would expect "at a minimum, large single-digit" percentage declines in US house prices from peak to trough[16] and added that he would not be surprised if the fall was "in double digits".

Mr. Greenspan said house prices were probably already down about 2–3 percent from their peak on a national level.

However, he cautioned[17] that it was very difficult to predict how large the ultimate decline would be.

As Fed chairman, Mr. Greenspan had talked about "froth" in the housing sector, but never said there was a bubble in the market as a whole. His successor Ben Bernanke has also avoided the word "bubble".

However, Mr. Greenspan told the FT that froth "was a euphemism[18] for a bubble". He said he still thought froth—a collection of bubbles—was a better description, because of the variation[19] in house price appreciation[20] in

险要比他在任时更大。

格林斯潘称，他预计美国房价从峰值水平到最低水平"至少会出现较大个位数"的跌幅，并补充说，如果跌幅"达到两位数"，他也不会感到惊讶。

格林斯潘表示，从全国水平看，房价可能已经较峰值水平下跌了2%至3%左右。

但他警告，很难预测最终跌幅会有多大。

在担任美联储主席期间，格林斯潘曾谈到房地产市场的"浮沫"，但从未表示房地产市场整体存在泡沫。他的继任者本·伯南克也避免使用"泡沫"这个词。

然而，格林斯潘日前在接受英国《金融时报》采访时表示，浮沫"是泡沫的委婉说法"。他表示，他仍然认为浮沫（由小泡沫堆积而成）是更好的表述，因为美国

---

[15] resurgence [ri'sə:dʒəns] n.苏醒，复活，恢复活力
[16] trough [trɔ(:)f] n.商业周期的低潮
[17] caution ['kɔ:ʃən] v.警告，告诫
[18] euphemism ['ju:fimizəm] n.[语]委婉语，委婉法
[19] variation [ˌvɛəri'eiʃən] n.变化，变动，变更
[20] appreciation [əˌpri:ʃi'eiʃən] n.涨价，增值

different local housing markets. But he said "all the froth bubbles add up to an aggregate bubble".

The former chairman said the current turmoil[21] in financial markets was "an accident waiting to happen".

He said the price of risk had fallen to unsustainably[22] low levels beforehand, with investors addicted to asset[23]-backed securities that offered some additional yield over Treasury bonds as if they were "cocaine[24]".

各地房地产市场上的房价涨幅各不相同。但他表示："这些浮沫聚集在一起，就会形成一个总体的泡沫。"

这位美联储前主席称，当前的金融市场动荡是"一件迟早要发生的事"。

他表示，此前风险价格降到了不可持续的低位，对于能够提供比美国国库券更高收益率的资产支持证券，投资者就好像吸了"可卡因"一样上瘾。

---

[21] turmoil ['tə:mɔil] *n.*骚动，混乱
[22] unsustainably *ad.* 不可持续地
[23] asset ['æset] *n.*财产，资产
[24] cocaine [kə'kein] *n.*[药]可卡因

非常点拨

1. Treasury bonds，（长期）国库券，是政府为筹集国家建设资金而面向社会公众发行的一种中央政府债券。由于国库券的投资风险极低，可获得较好的投资收益，因此是个人理财的优秀品种。

2. *The Financial Times*, 英国《金融时报》，全球领先的财经报纸，其权威性、真实性和准确性深受认可。该报纸在全球23个城市为读者提供大量的新闻、评论和分析信息，日发行量44万份，全球共有超过140万名读者。

英国《金融时报》

Jim Rogers

Unit 4

Jim Rogers
投资骑士：吉姆·罗杰斯

主题札记

吉姆·罗杰斯是第三位介绍量子基金的核心人物，也是最为潇洒的一位，他一边环球旅行，一边投资，这就是量子基金创始人之一、人称"奥地利股市之父"、周游列国并进行全球投资的吉姆·罗杰斯。

吉姆·罗杰斯（Jim Rogers）是在1997年令东南亚国家闻风丧胆的"量子基金"的前合伙人，是国际著名的投资家和金融学教授。曾被Jon Train's《现代投资大师》、Jack Schwager's《市场奇才》等著名年鉴收录。罗杰斯还是《时代周刊》（*Time*）、《华盛顿邮报》（*The Washington Post*）、《纽约时报》（*The New York Times*）、《巴伦周刊》（*Barron's*）、《福布斯》（*Forbes*）、《财富》（*Fortune*）、《华尔街日报》（*The Wall Street Journal*）和《金融时报》（*The Financial Times*）的长期撰稿人。

阅读长廊

Investment Biker:
Jim Rogers

Jim B.Rogers, Jr. (born on October 19,1942) is an American investor and financial commentator. He is co-founder, along with George Soros, of the Quantum Fund, and is a college professor, author, world traveler, economic commentator, and creator of the Rogers International Commodities Index (RICI).

One of the nation's most acclaimed[1] and successful financial experts, Rogers grew up in Demopolis, Alabama. He got started in business at the age of six, selling peanuts and soft drinks at Little League games. He graduated from Yale University and studied philosophy, politics and economics at Oxford University, where he discovered his love for Wall Street and investing.

After a spectacular[2] career as a hedge fund

投资骑士：
吉姆·罗杰斯

吉姆·罗杰斯（生于1942年10月19日），美国著名的投资家和金融评论家。他和索罗斯一起创立了量子基金。罗杰斯是一名大学教授、作家、世界旅行家、经济评论家，也是罗杰斯国际商品指数的创立者。

作为全国最受拥戴的、最成功的金融专家之一，罗杰斯在阿拉巴马州迪莫波利斯长大。六岁时他就开始做生意，在青年联赛上出售花生和饮料。他从耶鲁大学毕业之后又去牛津大学学习哲学、政治学和经济学，在那里，他发现了自己对华尔街和投资的热爱。

作为对冲基金经理和投资大

---

[1] acclaim [əˈkleim] *v.* 以欢呼声拥戴（或推举、承认）
[2] spectacular [spekˈtækjulə] *a.* 引人注意的；惊人的

manager and investor, Rogers is sometimes a visiting professor at Columbia University. He is a regular contributor to *Worth* magazine and a business correspondent for Fox News, in addition to CNBC. His forecasts are featured in *Barron's*, *Fortune*, *The Wall Street Journal*, *The Financial Times*, *Time*, *The Washington Post* and many other domestic and international publications.

Jim Rogers was a Wall Street legend long before he wrote his first best seller, *Investment Biker*. In the 1970's, he made what he describes as "more money than I knew existed in the world", managing the Quantum Fund, earning profiles[3] in such books as *The New Money Masters*, *Market Wizards* and *Money Masters of Our Time*. Since retiring at age 37, he has invested his own funds, been a finance professor at Columbia University, hosted television programs on WCBS, FNN and CNBC, and written columns for *Worth and Men's Journal*.

But Rogers is also renowned for being cut from a different cloth than most people on Wall Street. Not satisfied with an earlier record-setting trip around the world atop a motorcycle, for which *Time* called him the "Indiana Jones of finance", Rogers embarked with his fiancée,

师，在事业上取得惊人成绩后，罗杰斯有时也去哥伦比亚大学担任客座教授。他是商业杂志《价值》的固定投稿者，除了CNBC，他也是福克斯新闻的商务记者。他的预报成为一些杂志的特色，比如《巴伦周刊》、《财富》、《华尔街日报》、《金融时报》、《时代周刊》、《华盛顿邮报》以及很多国内和国际出版物。

吉姆·罗杰斯在写完他的第一本畅销书《投资骑士》之前，就已经是华尔街传奇人物。在20世纪70年代，据他自己描述，他挣了"比他所知道的世界上现存的钱还要多"的钱，管理量子基金，并被《现代投资大师》、《市场奇才》以及《我们时代的投资大师》等收录。自从37岁退休以来，他投资他自己的基金，成为哥伦比亚大学的金融学教授，主持WCBS（纽约的一个电台）、FNN和CNBC的电视节目，还为《财富与男人》写专栏文章。

但是罗杰斯还因为跟大多数华尔街的人不一样而闻名。他的第一次创纪录的骑摩托车环球旅行，被《时代周刊》称为"金融界的印地安纳·琼斯"，他似乎还不满足于此，在世纪之交——1999—2001年，又和他的未婚妻派吉·帕克尔

---

3 profile ['prəufail] *n.*传略，人物简介

Paige Parker, and a one-of-a-kind Mercedes Benz, on a new adventure to chronicle the world during the turn of the Millennium—1999–2001. They completed the 116-country, 152,000-mile overland trip, setting another Guinness World Record and getting married along the way. Rogers writes about his amazing travels and discoveries in *Adventure Capitalist: How I Drove Around the World for Three Years in a Yellow Mercedes, Visited 116 Countries, Invested Globally, Set a Guinness World Record, and Ate an Iguana*, which was published in Spring 2003. His other books include *Hot Commodities: How Anyone Can Invest Profitable in the World's Best Market* and the latest one, *A Bull in China*, released in December 2007.

Roger's previous trip around the world was no less impressive. As a small-town southern boy (his hometown was so small that his family's phone number was just "5") with a passion for motorcycling, Rogers had always dreamed of taking a trip around the world on his bike. In 1990 he did just that, setting out not only to travel, but to learn about the world's developing countries and investment markets first hand. It took nearly two years, but he drove 65,067 miles on land and traveled thousands more by sea, air, barge and rail across six continents, setting a world record for land travel along the way. *Investment Biker* was the story of this extraordinary trip and the world economy—

一起，开着奔驰系列的一款车，开始了他们的环球冒险。他们共到达116个国家，横越大陆152,000英里，创了又一项吉尼斯世界纪录，而且还在旅行途中结了婚。他把他的传奇经历写进了他的书《资本家的冒险》：我是怎样开着一辆黄色奔驰在三年内环游世界，参观访问116个国家，在全球投资，创造吉尼斯世界纪录，吃一只鬣蜥的。这本书已于2003年春天出版。他写的其他的书还包括《热门商品投资：怎样在世界上最好的市场中投资获利》，还有一本新书——《中国牛市》，2007年12月出版发行。

罗杰斯的前一次环球之旅也是很让人难忘的。他来自南方的一个小城（他的家乡是很小的一个地方，以至他们家的电话号码只有5位数），他非常喜欢骑摩托。罗杰斯一直梦想着有一天他能骑摩托车环游世界。1990年，他真的开始旅行，出发时想这不仅仅是旅行，而且可以了解世界上的发展中国家和投资市场，并获得第一手资料。那次旅行花了近两年的时间，但是他陆路旅行65,067英里，并乘船、飞机、游艇、火车经过成千上万英里的路程，穿越6个大洲，仅是沿途所经过陆路的长度，就创下了世界纪录。《投资骑士》这本书就是关于他的这次特殊的旅行和世界经济

getting to the heart of what drives successful nations and economies upward and what sends troubled ones downward.

During both of his exhilarating[4] trips, Rogers talked to businessmen, bankers, investors and local citizens in order to get a better sense of each country's infrastructure[5] and investment possibilities. It's no wonder, then, that he has racked up[6] huge profits in markets that Wall Street didn't know existed; unlike most people, he actually visits these places before he invests.

In Sep. 2007, Rogers sold his mansion in New York City for about 15 million USD and moved to Singapore. This is due mainly in his belief that this is a ground-breaking time for investment potential in Asian markets. Rogers' daughter is being tutored in Mandarin to prepare her for the future, he says. "Moving to Singapore and Dubai now is like moving to New York City in 1908," he said. Also, he is quoted to say: "If you were smart in 1807 you moved to London, if you were smart in 1907 you moved to New York City, and if you are smart in 2007 you move to Asia." In an CNBC interview with Maria Bartiromo broadcast on May 5, 2008, Rogers said that people in Asia are extremely motivated and driven, and he wants to be in that type of environment to be himself motivated and

的，该书透彻分析了促使成功国家经济上升的原因和导致一些国家经济滞后的原因。

在这两次激动人心的旅行中，为了更好地了解每个国家的基础设施和投资可能性，罗杰斯与商人、银行家、投资者和当地群众交谈。这不足为奇，那时他已经在市场上获得了华尔街都不知道的巨额利润；他和其他的很多人都不一样，在他投资前，他确确实实去过那些地方，有亲身经历和感性认识。

2007年9月，罗杰斯以1,500万美元卖了他在纽约的豪宅，搬到了新加坡。正是因为他相信对于亚洲市场的投资潜力来说，现在是创业的时候了。罗杰斯让女儿学习中文，为她将来的发展做准备，他说："搬到新加坡和迪拜就如同1908年的时候搬到纽约去住。"而且，据他讲，"如果1807年时你很聪明的话，你会搬到伦敦去；1907年时你很聪明的话，你会搬到纽约去；2007年时你很聪明的话，你会搬到亚洲去"。在2008年5月5日接受CNBC电视台记者玛丽亚·巴蒂罗摩采访时，罗杰斯说，亚洲人目的特别明确，并且很有动力，他希望在那种环境下他自己也能变得目的明确，有动力。在那次采访中，他还说，这正是美国和欧洲过去的

---

[4] exhilarate [ig'ziləreit] vt. 使高兴；使活跃；使振奋
[5] infrastructure ['infrə,strʌktʃə] n.基础；（社会、国家的）基础结构（如教育、运输、通信等设施）
[6] rack up [俚] 获（胜）、得（分）

driven. He said during that interview that, this is how America and Europe used to be. He chose not to move to Hong Kong or Shanghai due to the high levels of pollution causing potential health problems for his daughter.

样子。他没有选择移居到香港或者上海，是因为这些城市污染比较严重，可能会对他女儿的健康不利。

财经宝库

1. *Investment Biker*，《投资骑士》，著名投资大师、量子基金创始人、畅销书《热门商品投资》作者吉姆·罗杰斯的经典力作。本书是吉姆·罗杰斯在20世纪90年代初写的一本非常具有影响力与知名度的经典著作。在书中，作者描写了自己用了22个月的时间，骑摩托车环游世界，横跨6大洲52个国家和地区，考察当地投资环境时的所见、所闻、所感。本书语言通俗、情节生动，充满了幽默与智慧，对当地投资情况和未来发展的分析深入透彻，可读性强，是一部不可多得的睿智之作。

2. Guinness World Record，吉尼斯世界纪录。"吉尼斯"原是一家啤酒厂的名字，吉尼斯世界纪录的产生出于一次偶然争论。一天，酿造厂经理比佛在打猎时，突然看见一只从未见过的飞鸟。大家便开始议论这种鸟是不是欧洲飞得最快的鸟，但找不到文字记载，最后只好不了了之。不过，比佛没有放弃。1954年9月12日，他与孪生兄弟成立了一个专门收集世界之最的机构，取名为吉尼斯公司，并马上开始了编写工作。1955年8月7日，第一本《吉尼斯世界纪录大全》正式出版，2004年，吉尼斯迎来了它的50岁生日。

3. Indiana Jones，印地安纳·琼斯，是电视剧《少年印地安纳·琼斯大冒险》的主人公，该剧于1992年在美国ABC电视台首播，根据著名系列电影《夺宝奇兵》改编，讲述了少年印地安纳·琼斯从10岁起和他父亲一起环游世界的神奇冒险经历。该剧拍摄地点包括全球众多国家：英国、俄罗斯、西班牙、捷克、斯洛伐克、肯尼亚、法国、印度、中国、澳大利亚、埃及、美国、摩洛哥、爱尔兰、意大利、土耳其、希腊和泰国。

4. *Hot Commodities*，《热门商品投资》，吉姆·罗杰斯的经典力作，这是一本实用的投资建议方面的书。在这本书中，罗杰斯认为，当前世界范围的商品供需紊乱——这是典型的商品投资市场接近长期牛市的信号。这场牛市早已悄无声息地在我们身边开始了，而且还将持续10年。罗杰斯从商品的供给和需求出发，深入分析了石油、黄金、铅、糖、咖啡等商品的历史及未来走势，深入浅出，他的建议无疑为深陷股市泥潭的投资者指出了一条光明大道。

5. *A Bull in China*，《中国牛市》，吉姆·罗杰斯著，在本书中，著名投资大师吉姆·罗杰斯对中国的农业、工业、商业、能源、交通、旅游、健康、科教、房地产等重要行业二十多年来的发展状况以及未来的走势进行了深入而透彻的分析，对这些领域中具有投资潜力的上市公司也进行了独具慧眼的点评和推荐。该书堪称投资者把握中国未来投资市场、获得长期收益的经典必读书。

6. CNBC电视台，该电视台是美国全国广播公司（NBC）旗下的财经频道。自2004年美国有线广播电视公司（CNN）关闭其财经频道CNNfn以来，CNBC在财经新闻领域就一直占据主导地位。

DIY工作室

1. Please talk about Jim Rogers' two trips around the world.

2. Why did Jim Rogers choose to move to Singapore and live there?

归类记忆卡片

成本推进型 cost push　　　　　　　　　货币供应 money supply

本票 promissory notes	汇率机制 ERM
劳动力 labor force	储备货币 reserve currency
实际工资 real wages	劳动密集型 labor-intensive
最终目标 ultimate goal	股票交易所 bourse
坏的影响 adverse effect	回报率 rate of return
担保 ensure	牛市 bull market
贴现 discount	非凡的牛市 a raging bull
萧条的 sluggish	规模经济 scale economy
期货（股票）futures	买方出价与卖方要价之间的差价 bid-ask spreads
公共债务 membership criteria	

听力广场

Rogers warns of China bubble developing in mainland market

By Jamil Anderlini

Tuesday, October 30, 2007

Jim Rogers, the investor and author, has warned of an "incipient[7] bubble" in the mainland

罗杰斯警告中国内地股市泡沫正在扩散

投资者兼作家吉姆·罗杰斯（Jim Rogers）日前在接受采访时

---

[7] incipient [in'sipiənt] *a.* 开始的，刚出现的，早期的

Chinese stock market in an interview .

He is recommending investors should buy Hong Kong-listed shares in Chinese companies instead.

Mr. Rogers has been generating headlines in recent weeks with his bearish comments on the US and the dollar and his recommendation[8] to buy the Chinese renminbi.

But he acknowledged there were not a lot of options for foreign investors wanting to buy assets on the Chinese mainland.

"I wouldn't buy real estate and I know I wouldn't buy any (mainland-traded) A-shares now," he said. "I don't know why anybody would buy shares in Shanghai when you can buy them in Hong Kong at a big discount."

Thanks to a stock market that has increased nearly sixfold[9] in 28 months, China is now home to five of the world's 10 largest companies by market capitalization[10] compared with three for the US.

警告，中国内地股市正处于"泡沫初期阶段"。

他建议，投资者应当转而购买在香港上市交易的中国公司股票。

由于最近数周发表了看空美国经济和美元的言论，并建议投资者买进人民币，罗杰斯频频登上各大媒体头条。

但他承认，对于希望购买中国内地资产的外国投资者而言，选择并不多。

"我不会买房地产，我知道我现在也不会买（在内地交易的）A股，"他表示，"当人们能够以较高折价在香港买到中国公司股票时，我不明白为什么还会有人在上海买。"

由于中国股市在28个月内上涨了近6倍，目前在全世界市值最大的10家公司中，中国拥有5家，相比之下，美国只有3家。

---

[8] recommendation [ˌrekəmenˈdeiʃən] *n.*推荐、介绍
[9] sixfold *ad.*六倍、六重
[10] capitalization [kəˌpitəlaiˈzeiʃən] *n.*计算（某一时期内收益）的现在价值

Mr. Rogers says he is heavily invested in China and has never sold a single Chinese share in his life but, if the market continues to climb, he will have to consider selling out.

"It may sound strange for someone who owns Chinese shares to say it would be good for stocks to go down 30 or 40 percent but, if they don't, there'll be a bubble—and bubbles always end very badly," he said.

Another high-profile investor, Warren Buffett, recently sold the last of his shares in Petrochina, China's biggest petrochemical[11] firm and likely to become the largest company in the world when it begins trading in Shanghai in early November.

罗杰斯表示，他重仓持有中国公司股票，而且从未卖出过一股，但如果中国股市继续上涨，他将不得不考虑卖出。

他表示："如果持有中国公司股票的人说，中国股市下跌30%或40%是有益的，这可能听上去有些奇怪，但如果股市不下跌，就会产生泡沫——泡沫破裂的后果总是很严重。"

另一位著名投资者沃伦·巴菲特（Warren Buffett）最近出售了其持有的最后一部分中石油（Petrochina）股票。中石油是中国最大的石化公司，在其股票于11月初在上海证交所上市交易后，该公司有可能成为全球市值最大的公司。

---

[11] petrochemical [ˌpetrəuˈkemikəl] *a.*石油化学的

非常点拨

　　1. 沃伦·巴菲特（Warren Buffett），沃伦·巴菲特被喻为"当代最成功的投资者"。在历史上伟大的投资家中，巴菲特以他敏锐的业务评估技术引人注目。

Louis Bacon

Unit 5

Louis Bacon
对冲基金王者：路易斯·培根

主题札记

　　路易斯·培根，美国对冲基金经理，他非常擅长运用宏观策略在市场上投资。从1990年以来，他一直在最能挣钱的100名人中保持在前20位。他被认为是20世纪最有才能的100位交易商之一。据估计，他的现有净资产达17亿美元。

阅读长廊

Macro Money Maker

By Dyan Manchan

Louis Bacon (born in 1956) is an American hedge fund manager and commodities trader who uses a global macro strategy to invest in the markets. Bacon has been at the top 20 ranking of Top 100 money earners since the 1990s. He is considered one of the top 100 traders of the 20th century. With an estimated current net worth of around $1.7 billion, he is ranked by Forbes as the 707th richest person in the world. He is the manager of a leading New York City-based hedge fund, Moore Capital Management.

Bacon was a literature major at Middlebury College, One summer he captained a sport-fishing boat for Walter Frank, who had a seat on the New York Stock Exchange. He caught the bug. Entering Columbia Business School, he tried trading the proceeds of a low-interest loan he'd taken out for living expenses three terms in a row. He lost on sugar, cotton and gold contracts each time. Humbled, he had to go to

对冲基金王者
路易斯·培根：

路易斯·培根（生于1956年），是美国的对冲基金经理，是运用全球宏观策略在市场上投资的商品交易者。从20世纪90年代开始，他就在世界100个最能挣钱的人中排前20名。他被认为是20世纪100个最有名的交易者之一。估计他现在的净资产有17亿美元，在福布斯世界富豪榜排707位。他是纽约比较领先的对冲基金——摩尔资金管理公司的经理。

培根在米德伯瑞大学读的是文学专业。有一年夏天，他为纽约股票交易所的沃尔特·弗兰克的渔船当船长，从中颇有收获。进入哥伦比亚商学院后，他连续三个学期用生活费低息贷款来做投资交易，结果他每次都在糖、棉花、黄金交易上赔了钱，到头来不得不低声下气地向父亲要生活费。只有在第四学期他才开始赚钱。

his dad and ask for spending money. Only by the fourth and final term did he climb into the black.

Having earned his M.B.A., Bacon entered the Bankers Trust trading and sales program in 1981. "They took an instant dislike to me," says Bacon, "I thought I was too cool." His superior attitude brought him the equivalent[1] of a Siberian assignment—banker's acceptances. To further the insult this son of the South would have to work for a woman.

Back to work for fishing buddy[2] Walter Frank trading currencies in 1982, he lost some of the capital Frank fronted him. Still, Shearson Lehman hired him as a futures broker. Lucky for Bacon that his brother Zack, a trader at Soros' Quantum Fund, and his friend Jones both traded through his desk, making him a big producer.

By 1989 he was on his own. Jones wasn't accepting new money, so he recommended his clients invest in Moore. Bacon's first year proved his best; he correctly predicted the first Gulf war's impact on world oil prices and shorted the Nikkei index just before it collapsed. The fund was up 86%.

Secretive[3], risk-conscious, a bit paranoid[4]—

获得了MBA学位后，培根于1981年开始为银行家信托交易和销售项目工作。"他们一开始就不喜欢我，"培根说，"我认为我太孤傲了。"他的高傲态度使他只能去做银行承兑汇票工作——就像被发配到西伯利亚一样。更过分的是，这个南方青年要给一个女人打下手。

1982年，他又回头为捕鱼伙伴沃尔特·弗兰克做货币交易，把弗兰克给他的钱亏掉了一些。但席尔森·雷曼仍雇他做期货经纪商。幸运的是，担任索罗斯量子基金交易员的培根的哥哥萨克和培根的朋友琼斯两个人都与培根做交易，结果使培根成为一个大交易商。

1989年培根开始自立门户成立了摩尔公司。当时琼斯没有吸纳新资金，所以他就推荐他的客户投资于摩尔公司。第一年培根就干得非常出色，他正确预见了第一次海湾战争对世界石油价格的冲击，在日经指数崩盘前卖空。他的基金上升了86%。

路易斯·培根拥有许多对冲基

---

1 equivalent [i'kwivələnt] n. 相等物，等值物
2 buddy ['bʌdi] n.[美俚] 伙伴，弟兄（尤指兵士间称呼）
3 secretive [si'kri:tiv] a. 守口如瓶的；不坦率的
4 paranoid ['pærənɔid] a. （像）患妄想狂（或偏执狂）的

Louis Bacon has many of the traits of a hedge fund boss. A nice chunk[5] of the $7 billion he plays with is his own.

It's hard to know when hedge fund trader Louis Bacon, 48, of Moore Capital Management, first put up the walls that protect him from a cruel market and a crueler world. Could it have been when the kids in Raleigh, N.C. made fun of his schoolboy spectacles? "Glasses were an affront[6] to my youthful vanity," is how he sees it now. He took them off at school until his strict parents got wind of it.

Or was it when the mentor at whose knee he'd learned to trade commodities blew his brains out after a single mistake erased his net worth? Philip Hehmeyer, a free-wheeling Southerner, was a larger-than-life character on the New York Cotton Exchange. He was also short the S&P 500 Index before the August 1982 rally and took his life at 37 rather than face bankruptcy and public humiliation[7]. "I saw the utter agony and ruination[8] of sticking with a losing position," Bacon says.

Or could it have been in 1985, when Bacon first tried to run money for Commodities Corp., the firm that gave traders like Bruce

金经理共有的特性：神秘、对风险高度敏感，并且有点偏执狂。他所管理的70亿美元的资金是他自己的资产。

不知是在什么时候，现年48岁的摩尔资本管理公司的对冲基金经理路易斯·培根在残酷的市场和更残酷的世界面前第一次建立了一道防护墙。难道是幼年时北卡罗来纳州罗利的同伴们取笑他戴的眼镜时，这种意识就萌芽了么？"眼镜事件使我年轻的虚荣心受到了伤害"，培根现在这样评论。他在学校里摘掉了眼镜，但严厉的父母发现后制止了他。

抑或是他师从学习商品交易的导师菲利普·海默亚因为一个小错误而举枪自尽对他产生了重大影响。自由放任的南方人菲利普·海默亚是纽约棉花交易所的传奇人物，他曾在1982年8月股市回升之前卖空标准普尔500指数并且在37岁时结束了自己的生命，以免面对破产和公众的羞辱。"我看到了交易亏损带来的极度痛苦和毁灭"，培根如是说。

或者是另外一件事塑造了培根，1985年，他第一次为商品交易公司操盘就尝到了失败的苦果，当

---

[5] chunk [tʃʌŋk] *n.* 相当大的数量（或部分）
[6] affront [əˈfrʌnt] *n.* 当众侮辱
[7] humiliation [hju(ː)ˌmiliˈeiʃən] *n.* 羞辱，蒙耻
[8] ruination [ruiˈneiʃən] *n.* 毁灭、毁坏

Kovner their start, and got his own taste of ashes? Mortified[9] after losing a third of $100,000 in principal, he insisted on giving the balance back. Elaine Crocker, the Commodities Corp. Executive who funded traders, coaxed[10] him a couple years later to try again, Crocker, his ally and protector back then, has that job officially as the president of Moore Capital today.

Whatever shaped him, Bacon turned wariness[11] into might. Moore Capital (after his mother's maiden name) manages $7 billion out of New York and London. It's a trading powerhouse, and its founder a new member of The Forbes 400. Bacon is a global macro trader, a genre that includes George Soros, the Bush-hating billionaire, and Paul Tudor Jones. They storm into any moving market, be it a currency in an obscure[12] corner of the globe or stocks in wild and woolly[13] Moscow.

As well-known as Bacon is in trading circles, he's little-known outside of them. That's partly because he is good at controlling his own exposure, with suspicion that can verge on paranoia[14]. A former Moore employee recalls

时这家公司为如布鲁斯·科夫纳之类的交易员们提供起步资金。在亏损了自己掌握的10 万美元本金的三分之一后，羞愧的培根归还了剩余的资金罢手不干。为交易员提供资金的商品交易公司主管伊莱恩·科洛克两年后说服他东山再起。科洛克，当时培根的支持者和保护者，现在是摩尔资本管理公司的董事长。

无论是什么塑造了他，培根把谨慎转变为力量。摩尔资本（以他母亲结婚前娘家的姓命名）在纽约和伦敦管理70亿美元的资金，是一个交易的源泉，他的创始人是福布斯400富豪榜的新贵。培根进行的是全球宏观交易，从事此类交易者还包括憎恨布什总统的亿万富翁乔治·索罗斯以及保罗·都铎·琼斯。他们在变化莫测的市场中大显身手，无论是世界不起眼角落的某种货币或是未开化的莫斯科的股票都有可能成为他们的目标。

培根在圈内的知名度很高，但在圈外却鲜为人知。这部分是因为近乎偏执的猜疑心使他很善于控制自己的曝光率。摩尔公司的一位前雇员回想起1991年的一天，当时的

---

9 mortify ['mɔ:tifai] vt. 使受辱；伤害（别人的感情）
10 coax [kəuks] v.用好话劝；诱（出），哄（出）
11 wariness ['wɛərinis] n.谨慎，小心；警惕
12 obscure [əb'skjuə] a.不引人注目的，偏僻的
13 woolly ['wuli] a. [美] 粗旷的（指具有早期美国西部生活特色的）wild and wolly 粗野的
14 paranoia [,pærə'nɔiə] n. [医]妄想狂，偏执狂

a day in 1991 when James Kelly, Moore's president at the time, strolled through the office with a private detective who carried a box that had a TV-like antenna[15] and blinking lights, sweeping for bugs. Staffers won't even tell you whether Bacon's in town. He's serious about confidentiality[16] agreements and not above some intimidation[17]. "If I talk, only bad things can happen," says James Capra of hedge fund Capra Asset Management in New York.

As much as his privacy, Bacon craves[18] order and control. "As a speculator you must embrace[19] disorder and chaos," he explains. In the early 1990s he would have New York underlings[20] jet over hot-off-the-press Barron's copies on Friday; the boss liked to read it on Saturday.

But judging risk has become his calling card. Bacon's flagship offshore fund, Moore Global Investments, claims to have returned 24% annually (net of fees) since its inception in 1990, with a volatility[21] (annualized standard deviation of monthly returns) of 13%, well below the 15% you'd get on an S&P 500 Index fund. While Jones and Kovner both have funds

摩尔公司董事长詹姆斯·凯利和一名扛着装有如电视天线和闪烁信号灯的盒子的私家侦探在办公室里探测有没有装窃听器。公司职员连培根是否在城里都不会说。培根对保密性极为重视，担心会受到某些媒体的惊吓。"如果我说了，只有坏处没有好处，"纽约的对冲基金卡普拉资产管理公司的詹姆斯·卡普拉回忆道。

培根重视私密性，也同样渴望秩序和控制。他对此的解释是"作为一个投机者，你必须和无序混乱打交道"。在20世纪90年代初期，他让纽约的下属把刚印刷出版的《巴伦周刊》（美国财经杂志）在星期五快递到家里，因为他星期六要读。

判断风险已经变成了他的名片。培根的旗舰离岸基金，自摩尔全球投资1990年创立以来年回报率达24%（除去费用后），不稳定性（月收益率的年标准差）为13%，明显低于标准普尔500指数基金的15%。虽然琼斯和科夫纳的基金有更高的年收益率，但他们的投资组合的不稳定性更高。

---

[15] antenna [æn'tenə] *n.*天线
[16] confidentiality ['kɔnfi,denʃi'æləti] *n.*机密，秘密
[17] intimidation [in,timi'deiʃən] *n.*威胁，恐吓
[18] crave [kreiv] *vt.* 渴望，热望
[19] embrace [im'breis] *vt.* 看到，领会
[20] underling ['ʌndəliŋ] *n.* [贬]下属；下手
[21] volatility [,vɔlə'tiliti] *n.*易变；反复无常

with higher annualized returns, their portfolios[22] also have higher volatility.

On the global macro fund and half a dozen other Moore offerings, Bacon charges on the high side of an industry known for obscene[23] fees. His clients pay up to 3% annually plus up to 25% of profits. The minimum account sizes $5 million and client money is initially locked up for three years. "When someone multiplies your capital," says Antoine Bernheim of Dome Capital. A hedge fund advisory firm that's been a client for 15 years, "the last thing you do is complain about fees".

Today Bacon has a hedge fund king's trophies[24]: several boats, his own jet and two private polo fields. He has his own private island near a spread in the Hamptons, a 15,000-acre ranch in the Southwest near Ted Turner's, a house in the Bahamas, one in the Scottish countryside and, of course, a penthouse in Manhattan. He shares a home in London, his main base, with his fiancée and their child. His first marriage, to Cynthia Ingraham, gave him four kids and a divorce bill for more than $100 million in 2002. While there was animosity[25] on both sides, the divorce was quick and—blessedly for a privacy zealot—stayed out of the tabloids[26].

在全球宏观基金以及摩尔资本管理公司提供的其他多个基金产品中，培根收取的管理费是行业内比较高的，而此行业又以高昂管理费而著称。他的客户支付的年管理费率是3%，还有利润的25%归培根所有。客户的最低投资金额是500万美元，三年内不得赎回。多姆资本管理公司是对冲基金咨询公司，作为其客户已有15年，服务于此的安东尼·波恩海姆说："如果有人能让你的资金翻上几倍，你就不会抱怨管理费太高了。"

今天，培根享有对冲基金王者的荣耀。他拥有几艘私人游艇，自己的喷气式飞机，两块私人马球场。他还在哈姆顿拥有属于自己的岛屿，在西南有一个15,000英亩的牧场（离美国有线新闻网老板特纳的牧场很近），在巴哈马群岛有一所住宅，还有一所在苏格兰乡村，当然还有曼哈顿的公寓。伦敦是他的主要基地，他与未婚妻和他们的孩子住在一起。他的第一任妻子辛西娅·英格拉姆和他生了四个孩子，2002年离婚，他支付了1亿多美元。虽然双方互相憎恨，但离婚进行的迅速而隐秘，远离了小报记者的骚扰。

---

[22] portfolio [pɔ:t'fəuljəu] *n.* [商]有价证券
[23] obscene [ɔb'si:n] *a.*可憎的，令人厌恶的
[24] trophy ['trəufi] *n.*（体育比赛等的）奖杯；胜利纪念章
[25] animosity [ˌæni'mɔsiti] *n.* 仇恨，憎恶，敌意
[26] tabloid ['tæblɔid] *n.*（以轰动性报道为特点的、多图画的）小报

Unlike his friend Jones, whose star-studded Robin Hood nonprofit extravaganzas[27] attract frenzied[28] media coverage, Bacon's philanthropic activities are less visible. Conservation and land preservation are targets. This descendant of Indian fighter Nathaniel Bacon loves to hunt, especially with bow and arrow. He bought Long Island Sound's 435-acre Robins Island in 1993 for $11 million and the nearby 540-acre Cow Neck Farm in 1998 for $25 million. After land prices rose steadily in both places, he gave conservation easements[29] to the Nature Conservancy and the Peconic Land Trust. The resulting charitable deduction reclaimed several millions of dollars spent on the properties. A good trade.

不像他的朋友琼斯，喜欢以罗宾汉式的侠义行为吸引媒体报道，培根的慈善活动很不引人注意。环保和土地保护是主要内容。这个印第安武士纳萨尼尔·培根的后代喜欢打猎，特别是弓箭狩猎。1993年，他以1,100万美元买下了长岛海湾435英亩的罗宾斯岛，1998年以2,500万美元买下了附近的540英亩的考奈克农场。两处的土地价格稳步上升后，他把土地使用权交给了自然保护组织和派克尼克土地基金，所获得的几百万美元慈善性支出全部用来修建房屋。真是一笔好交易。

1. 本文摘自Forbes, Dec.27，2004。

2. 乔治·索罗斯，号称"金融天才"，从1969年建立量子基金至今，他创下了令人难以置信的业绩。

---

[27] extravaganza [eks,trævə'gænzə] *n.* 狂言；狂行
[28] frenzy ['frenzi] *vt.* [常用被动语态]使狂乱
[29] easement ['i:zmənt] *n.*附属建筑物

3. 保罗·都铎·琼斯，1976年从做经纪人起家，第二年就赚了100多万美元佣金。1980年，琼斯到纽约棉花交易所当现场交易员，几年之内赚了上千万美元。1984年琼斯离开交易所，创建都铎基金，从150万美元做起。4年后投资到都铎基金的每1,000美元已增值到1,700多美元。到1992年底，都铎基金总额已增长到60亿美元。1987年10月，世界上大部分投资者损失惨重。同一个月，保罗·都铎·琼斯掌管的都铎基金却获得62%的收益。琼斯的出色表现是一贯的，他曾经连续5年保持三位数的盈利增长，1992年底欧洲货币体系发生危机，琼斯数月内在外汇市场盈利十几亿美元。

4. *Barron's*，《巴伦周刊》，创刊于1921年，发行量超过30万份。作为专业财经周刊，《巴伦周刊》以帮助美国专业及机构投资者把握金融市场发展方向为宗旨，以准确的判断和透彻的分析为特色。

1. How do you understand Louis Bacon's traits as a hedge fund trader: secretive[30], risk-conscious, and a bit paranoid?

2. What do you think of Bacon's philanthropic activities?

交易员 dealer | 投资回收期 investment payoff period

---

[30] secretive [si'kri:tiv] *a.* 守口如瓶的；不坦率的

亏损 deficit	智力资本 intellectual capital
货币市场共同基金 money market mutual funds	网上银行业 online-banking
商业票据 commercial paper	账面收益 paper profit
过剩基金 surplus funds	产权清晰 clearly-established ownership
退出流通 out of circulation	筹资融资 fund and financing
违约风险 default risk	闲置的生产能力 spare capacity
养老基金 pension funds	转手贸易 switch trade
浮动比率 floating-rate	虚拟银行 virtual bank
资本市场 capital market	上市 go public

听力广场

The billionaire bought the ranch in Colorado

Fort Garland, Colorado? The Trinchera Ranch in the San Luis Valley has changed hands from a man worth almost $500 million to billionaire hedge-fund manager Louis Bacon.

Steve Forces said he had sold the 171,000-acre Forbes Trinchera Ranch near Fort Garland to Bacon because he had a solid conservation record and could be trusted to preserve the ranch.

亿万富翁买了科罗拉多州的牧场

加兰堡，科罗拉多州？在圣路易斯山谷的特里切拉牧场已易手，从一名身价5亿元的男子手里转移到了亿万富翁对冲基金经理路易斯·培根手中。

史蒂夫·弗西斯说，他已把17.1万英亩的加兰堡附近的福布斯特里切拉牧场卖给培根，因为他有可靠的土地保护的记录，并且可以被委托去维护牧场。

The Pueblo[31] Chieftain said Bacon paid $175 million for the ranch with views of 14,000-foot-high peaks, in one of the highest prices ever paid for a ranch. The Forbes family had held the ranch, 160 miles south of Denver, for four decades.

"Louis Bacon has passionately devoted much of his life and resources to the protection of extraordinary properties," Forbes said. "By finding such a committed[32] owner, we are certain Trinchera will thrive and be enjoyed, as it is, for years to come." Bacon set up the Moore Charitable Foundation in 1992 to aid nonprofit groups that focus primarily on conservation and the protection of natural resources.

A spokesman for Bacon called the ranch an extraordinary property for its scenic grandeur and unspoiled natural habitat.

The transaction[33] brings a close to the nearly four decades of ownership by the Forbes family.

Malcolm Forbes bought the ranch in 1969 and expanded it in 1982 with the purchase of the adjacent[34] Blanca Ranch. The Forbes family used the ranch as a hunting preserve, for corporate entertaining and as an executive

该印第安人的村庄首领说，培根支付1.75亿美元买牧场，因为牧场有14,000英尺高的山峰景观，这个价格可能是购买牧场的最高价格。福布斯家族在丹佛以南160英里左右拥有这个牧场，已经有40多年了。

"路易斯·培根积极投身于一些特殊财产的保护，"福布斯说，"找到了这样守信用的业主，我们敢肯定特里切拉牧场在未来的日子里，一定会像现在一样蓬勃发展的，他们会喜欢这里的。"1992年，培根成立了摩尔慈善基金会，用以资助那些旨在维护和保护自然资源的非营利性团体。

培根的发言人把牧场称做特殊财产，因为这里风景异常优美，并且是未受破坏的动物栖息地。

这笔交易也结束了福布斯对这个牧场近40年的所有权。

马尔科姆·福布斯在1969年买了这个牧场，1982年，又购买邻近的布兰卡的牧场，使原来的牧场规模扩大。福布斯家族把牧场作为一个狩猎禁地，当做社团娱乐和工作

---

[31] pueblo [pu'eblǝu] n. （美国西南部或墨西哥等）印地安人的村庄（或集体住所）
[32] commit [kǝ'mit] vt.使承担义务，使作出保证
[33] transaction [træn'zækʃǝn] n. （一笔）交易
[34] adjacent [ǝ'dʒeisǝnt] a. 邻近的，毗连的

retreat.

Bacon has made considerable donations to conservation causes, including the 1997 donation of a conservation easement to the Nature Conservancy[35] for Robins Island, a 434-acre property on the south shore of Long Island.

He guaranteed protection from development for the 540-acre Cow Neck Farm in the town of Southampton, N.Y., by donating a conservation easement to the Peconic Land Trust in 2001. Bacon's spokesman said he has no specific plans yet for Trinchera. He will keep the employees on, and may add some. There are an estimated 30 staff.

It wasn't clear whether the purchase included 80,000 acres that Forbes had given a conservation easement on in 2004 to Colorado Open Lands, the largest such donation in Colorado history.

The ranch is the largest remaining undeveloped land parcel within the historic Sangre de Cristo land grant of 1843.

休闲的场所。

培根为自然资源的保护捐了大笔款项，包括1997年为罗宾斯岛自然保护区捐款保护附属地，还有长岛南岸的434英亩的地产。

2001年，他捐款给自然保护组织派克尼克土地基金，保证保护纽约州南安普敦城540英亩的考奈克农场不受发展的影响。培根的发言人说，他还没有关于特里切拉的具体计划。他会保留原来的雇员，并可能会增加一些。估计有30名工作人员。

但我们并不清楚这次购买是否包括福布斯在2004年送给科罗拉多开放土地基金的8万英亩保护地，这在科罗拉多州的历史上是最大的一次捐赠。

这个牧场是1843年有历史意义的"基督圣血山"（Sangre de Cristo，西班牙语）政府赠与地中现存的未开发的最大的一片土地。

---

[35] conservancy [kənˈsəːvənsi] *n.* （渔场、森林等自然资源的）管理，保护；资源保护区

非常点拨

1. 本文来源：Associated Press（美联社）。

2. Sangre de Cristo，美国科罗拉多州基督圣血山，位于洛基山脉的南端，这是西班牙语，是"基督圣血"的意思。

美国科罗拉多州基督圣血山

George Soros

Unit 6

George Soros
金融大鳄：乔治·索罗斯

主题札记

　　乔治·索罗斯号称"金融天才"，从1969年建立量子基金至今，他创下了令人难以置信的业绩，以平均每年35％的综合成长率令华尔街同行望尘莫及。他好像具有一种超能的力量左右着世界金融市场。他的一句话就可以使某种商品或货币的交易行情突变，市场的价格随着他的言论上升或下跌。一名电视台的记者曾对此作出如此形象的描述：索罗斯投资于黄金，正因为他投资于黄金，大家都认为应该投资黄金，于是黄金价格上涨；索罗斯写文章质疑德国马克的价值，于是德国马克汇价下跌；索罗斯投资于伦敦的房地产，那里房产价格颓势在一夜之间得以扭转。索罗斯成功的秘密是许多人都急切想知道的，但由于索罗斯对其投资方面的事守口如瓶，这更给他蒙上了一层神秘的色彩。

阅读长廊

George Soros: the financial crocodile

By Charlotte Denny

George Soros (born August 12, 1930, in Budapest, Hungary) is a Hungarian-born American financial speculator, stock investor, philanthropist, and political activist.

In the United States, he is known for having donated large sums of money in a failed effort to defeat President George W. Bush's bid for re-election in 2004. On BookTV, November 12, 2007, he said that he supports Barack Obama for the Democratic candidate in the 2008 election, but says that John Edwards, Hillary Clinton, or Joe Biden are all fine candidates, as well.

George Soros is the son of the (Esperanto-language) writer Tivadar Schwartz. Tivadar was a Hungarian Jew, who was a prisoner of war during and after World War I and eventually escaped from Russia to rejoin his family in Budapest.

金融大鳄：乔治·索罗斯

乔治·索罗斯（1930年8月12日出生于匈牙利首都布达佩斯）是一位匈牙利出生的美国金融投机家，股票投资者，慈善家和政治活动积极分子。

在美国，他以捐助大量资金试图阻止2004年乔治·布什的再次当选而闻名。2007年11月12日在图书电视节目上，他说他支持巴拉克·奥巴马作为2008年民主党派总统候选人，但是他又说约翰·爱德华兹，希拉里·克林顿或者乔·拜登都是很好的候选人。

乔治·索罗斯的父亲是世界语作家蒂瓦达·斯瓦兹。蒂瓦达是匈牙利犹太人，是第一次世界大战的战俘，最后从俄罗斯逃出，回到他在布达佩斯的家中与家人团聚。

The family changed its name in 1936 from Schwartz to Soros, in response to growing anti-semitism with the rise of Fascism. Tivadar liked the new name because it is a palindrome and because it has a meaning. Although the specific meaning is left unstated in Kaufmann's biography, in Hungarian, "soros" means "next in line, or designated successor", and in Esperanto, it means "will soar"

George Soros wants to be the Bono of the financial world. The speculator whose assault[1] on sterling[2] ejected[3] Britain from the European exchange rate mechanism that September of 10 years ago has a mission—to use his estimated £5 billion fortune and his fame to help tackle what he sees as the failures of globalization. The idea that a man who made billions betting on the financial markets sides with the anti-globalization movement might strike some as ironic. Soros is clearly genuinely appalled[4] at the damage wrought on vulnerable[5] economies by the vast sums of money which flow across national borders every day.

"The US governs the international system to protect its own economy. It is not in charge

1936年，随着法西斯主义的兴起，反犹太主义的倾向日益明显，他们家把姓从斯瓦兹改成索罗斯。蒂瓦达喜欢这个新的姓氏，因为从拼写上看它是一个回文（指顺读和倒读都一样的词语），而且还有特别的意思。虽然在考夫曼的传记里并没有明确提及这个姓的含义，但是在匈牙利语里，"索罗斯"指"下一个"或者"指定继承人"，在世界语里，它意为"将要高飞，将要翱翔"。

乔治·索罗斯想成为金融界的博诺（U2乐队主唱）。这位在10年前的那个9月份攻击英镑迫使英国退出欧洲汇率机制的投机商有一项使命——利用他大约50亿英镑的财产和他的名声来帮助解决他所认为的全球化失败问题。一个靠在全球金融市场上的投机赚了几十亿英镑的人会支持反全球化运动，这对许多人来说是具有讽刺意义的。很明显，对于每天在各国之间流动的大量资金给经济脆弱国家造成的伤害，索罗斯从心底感到震惊。

索罗斯说："美国管理国际经济体系是为了保护本国经济，它并

---

[1] assault [ə'sɔ:lt] n.（武力或口头上的）攻击，袭击
[2] sterling ['stə:liŋ] n.英国货币
[3] eject [i(:)'dʒekt] v. 逐出，驱逐
[4] appall [ə'pɔ:l] v. 使吃惊，使丧胆
[5] vulnerable ['vʌlnərəbl] a.易受伤的，脆弱的

of protecting other economies," he says. "So when America goes into recession, you have anti-recessionary policies. When other countries are in recession, they don't have the ability to engage in anti-recessionary policies because they can't have a permissive monetary policy, because money would flee." In person, he has the air of a philosophy professor rather than a gimlet-eyed[6] financier. In a soft voice which bears the traces of his native Hungary, he argues that it is time to rewrite the so-called Washington consensus[7]—the cocktail of liberalization, privatization and fiscal rectitude[8] which the IMF has been preaching for 15 years. Developing countries no longer have the freedom to run their own economies, he argues, even when they follow perfectly sound policies. He cites Brazil, which although it has a floating currency and manageable public debt was paying ten times over the odds to borrow from capital markets.

Soros, who at one stage after the fall of the Berlin Wall was providing more assistance to Russia than the US government, believes in practicing what he preaches[9]. His Open Society Institute has been pivotal[10] in helping

不负责保护其他经济体。因此，当美国陷入衰退后，美国会出台反衰退政策。而其他国家陷入衰退时，却无力这样做，因为这些国家不能实行自由开放的货币政策，否则资金就会外流。"索罗斯本人并不像一个目光敏锐的金融家，他更具有哲学教授的气质。带着匈牙利母语口音，他轻声地说，现在是修改所谓的"华盛顿共识"的时候了。他指的是国际货币基金组织15年来宣扬的自由化、私有化和财政透明的综合体制。他说，发展中国家即使执行非常稳健的政策，也不能自由地控制本国经济。他援引巴西的例子说，尽管巴西实行了浮动汇率制和可控国债，但它向资本市场借款还是付出了比正常条件下高出10倍的成本。

索罗斯在柏林墙倒塌后一段时间内向俄罗斯提供的援助曾一度超过美国政府的援助。他坚定地实施自己宣扬的观点。他的"开放社会研究所"在帮助东欧国家发展民主

---

[6] gimlet-eyed *a.* 目光锐利的
[7] consensus [kən'sensəs] *n.* （意见等的）一致，合意
[8] rectitude ['rektitju:d] *n.* 正直，严正
[9] preach [pri:tʃ] *v.* 鼓吹
[10] pivotal ['pivətəl] *a.* 中枢的，枢要的，关键性的

eastern European countries develop democratic societies and market economies. Soros has the advantage of an insider's knowledge of the workings of global capitalism, so his criticism is particularly pointed. Last year, the Soros foundation's network spent nearly half a billion dollars on projects in education, public health and promoting democracy, making it one of the world's largest private donors.

Soros credits the anti-globalization movement for having made companies more sensitive to their wider responsibilities. "I think (the protesters) have made an important contribution by making people aware of the flaws of the system," he says. "People on the street had an impact on public opinion and corporations which sell to the public responded to that." Because the IMF has abandoned billion dollar bailouts[11] for troubled economies, he thinks a repeat of the Asian crisis is unlikely. The fund's new "tough love" policy—for which Argentina is the guinea pig—has other consequences. The bailouts were a welfare system for Wall Street, with western taxpayers rescuing the banks from the consequences of unwise lending to emerging economies. Now the IMF has drawn a line in the sand, credit to poor countries is drying up. "It has

社会和市场经济方面发挥了重要作用。索罗斯具有业内人士的优势，了解全球资本主义的运行，因此他的批评会特别尖锐。去年，索罗斯基金网络在教育、公共卫生、促进民主项目上花费了近5亿美元，使索罗斯基金成为世界上最大的私人捐助集团之一。

索罗斯赞扬反全球化运动使各公司更加认识到自己更广泛的责任。他说："我认为（反对者们）作出了重要贡献，使大众意识到这个体系的缺陷。大街上的人们对舆论会有所影响，而向公众推销商品的公司也会对舆论作出反应。"由于国际货币基金组织已经拒绝向经济困难的国家提供10亿美元的救济，索罗斯认为亚洲经济危机不会重演。国际货币基金组织"既爱又严"的新政策——阿根廷是该政策的试验品——带来了其他后果。西方纳税人挽救了银行因不理智地向新兴国家提供贷款造成的恶

这是位于美国华盛顿的国际货币基金组织总部大楼

---

11 bailout ['beilaut] n.紧急（财政）援助

created a new problem—the inadequacy[12] of the flow of capital from centre to the periphery[13]," he says.

The one economy Soros is not losing any sleep about is the US."I am much more positive about the underlying economy than I am about the market, because we are waging[14] war not only terrorism but also on recession," he says. "Although we don't admit it, we are actually applying Keynesian remedies, and I am a confirmed Keynesian. I have not yet seen an economy in recession when you are gearing up for war." He worries that the world's largest economic power is not living up to its responsibilities. "I would like the United States to live up to the responsibilities of its hegemonic[15] power because it is not going to give up its hegemonic power, "he says."The only thing that is realistic is for the United States to become aware that it is in its enlightened self-interest to ensure that the rest of the world benefits from their role."

果，而国际货币基金组织的那些救济金则成了华尔街的福利制度。现在国际货币基金组织对贫困国家的贷款正在枯竭。索罗斯说："这就产生了一个新问题——资金从中心向周边流动不足。"

索罗斯最不担心的就是美国经济。他说："我对美国的经济潜力比对现在的市场更有信心，因为我们正在进行的战争不仅是对付恐怖主义，而且也是在向经济衰退开战。尽管我们不承认，但我们实际是在奉行凯恩斯主义药方，我是一个坚定的凯恩斯主义者。我从来没见过哪个国家在准备战事时还会陷入经济衰退。"他担心这个世界上最大的经济大国不能承担起自己的责任。他说："我希望美国能够承担起作为霸权国家的职责，因为美国不会放弃自己的霸权地位。唯一现实的是，美国应意识到，保证世界上其他国家能从他们自己所承担的角色中受益，显然是符合美国自身利益的。"

---

[12] inadequacy [in'ædikwəsi] *n.*不充足，不适当
[13] periphery [pə'rifəri] *n.*边缘，周围，外围
[14] wage [weidʒ] *vt.* 开展（运动）；进行（斗争）
[15] hegemonic [,hi:gi'mɔnik] *a.*霸权的；统治的

财经宝库

1. anti-globalization movement，反全球化运动，是一种由不同团体人士发起的运动，他们各自从不同层面出发，都不约而同地认为全球化只会给当地社会及全世界带来恶果。一般而言，反全球化运动的示威者都被视为有社会主义甚至共产主义色彩。

2. the Berlin Wall，环绕西柏林的一道围墙。民主德国政府根据人民议院1961年8月12日通过的法令，于8月12日至8月13日夜间修筑。目的是制止民主德国居民（包括熟练技工）大量流入联邦德国。原为铁蒺藜围成的路障，后改筑成两米高、顶上拉着带刺铁丝网的混凝土墙。在正式的交叉路口和沿线的观察塔楼上设置警卫。1970年，虽然两德之间关系有所改善，民主德国政府还是把柏林墙加高到3米以阻止居民逃向西方。到1980年，围墙、电网和堡垒总长达1,369千米。除筑墙外还严格限制两德之间的人口流动。后根据两德政府于1971年12月20日签署的协议，限制略有放宽。1989年下半年，东欧各国政局剧变，民主德国在向德国西部移民浪潮的冲击下，于同年 11 月9日，将存在28年零3个月的柏林墙推倒，促进了德国的统一。

3. IMF，国际货币基金组织，全称是International Monetary Fund，它是政府间国际金融组织。1945年12月27日正式成立，1947年3月1日开始工作，1947年11月15日成为联合国的专门机构，在经营上有其独立性，总部设在华盛顿。按照惯例，国际货币基金组织总裁由欧洲人担任。

DIY工作室

1. Say something about the Quantum Fund started by George Soros and Jim Rogers.

2. Can you make comments on Soros' philanthropic efforts worldwide?

归类记忆卡片

现金外流 cash drains
经济人佣金 brokerage fee
大额定期存单（certificate of deposit, CD）
营业额 turnover
资本市场 capital market
布雷顿森林体系 The Bretton Woods System
经常账户 current account
套利者 arbitrager
远期汇率 forward exchange rate
即期汇率 spot rate

货币政策工具 tools of monetary policy
银行倒闭 bank failures
跨国公司 MNC（Multi-National Corporation）
商业银行 commercial bank
商业票据 comercial paper
利润 profit
本票，期票 promissory notes
监督 monitor
佣金（经济人） commission （brokers）
套期保值 hedge

听力广场

George Soros (1930–)

1. Introduction

The Soros family was Jewish and survived
the Nazi regime in Budapest during the Second

乔治·索罗斯

1. 简介

索罗斯家族是犹太人，在第二
次世界大战期间用假名和假身份证

World War by using false names and identity papers. As a student at the LSE George Soros was influenced by the British philosopher Karl Popper, who argued that Communism and Fascism were philosophically linked and who championed the open, democratic system (Hedges 1990).

Soros is active on a number of boards, including Fairchild Industries, Helsinki Watch, Americas Watch, the International League for Human Rights, the Brookings Council. His philanthropies[16] include the Open Society Inc., The Soros Foundation, the Fund for Reform and Opening of China Inc., and the Glasnost Foundation Inc.. He has received honorary doctoral degrees from the New School for Social Research, the University of Oxford, the Budapest University of Economics and Yale University. In addition, he was awarded the Laruea Honoris Causa by the University of Bologna for his global efforts to promote democratic societies.

Soros is "an intellectual who could discuss finances in five languages while turning his clients' investments into fortunes". He enjoys playing chess and philosophical debates. He has three children with his first wife, whom he broke up with in 1978 and divorced in 1981.

逃过了布达佩斯的纳粹当局。在伦敦经济学院就读时，索罗斯受到了英国哲学家卡尔·波普的影响，波普认为共产主义和法西斯主义在哲学上是联系在一起的，并支持公开民主的制度。

索罗斯在许多委员会上非常活跃，这当中包括：仙童产业，赫尔辛基观察，美洲观察，国际人权联盟和布鲁金斯委员会。他的慈善事业包括开放社会有限公司，索罗斯基金会，中国改革开放基金和格拉斯诺斯特基金。他从以下学习得到了名誉博士学位：新社会研究学院，牛津大学，布达佩斯经济大学和耶鲁大学，除此之外，他还因他的全球推动民主社会的努力而被波隆格那大学授予荣誉。

索罗斯是"一个在将客户的投资变成财富的同时，能用五种语言讨论金融问题的知识分子"。他喜欢下棋和哲学性的辩论。他与第一任妻子生育了三个小孩，1978年分居，1981年离婚。他的慈善事业

---

[16] philanthropy [fi'lænθrəpi] n. 善行；慈善性赠与物；慈善事业

His philanthropic activities began after his 1981 divorce. In 1983 he married Susan Weber, an art historian who is twenty-five years younger than him, The couple have two sons and maintain homes in Manhattan, Long Island and Bedford, New York, as well as London, England.

2. Main contribution

Soros spends two-thirds of his time and half of his annual income on promoting democracy abroad and a more tolerant society in the United States. In 1992 Soros contributed $100 million to support scientists and scientific research in Russia and the former Soviet countries. The donation was made by Soros in an attempt to slow the "brain drain" which was occurred since the break-up of the Soviet Union and to create What he hopes will become the equivalent of the National Science Foundation in the United States. Also in 1992,Soros provided Bosnian civilians with $50 million to help alleviate their suffering, Soros now runs foundations on 18 central and east European countries that support educational, cultural and economic activities. His contributions have funded Oxford scholarships for Hungarian, Polish and Soviet students. Worldwide, his philanthropic efforts in 1997 employed 1,300 people in twenty-four countries coordinated[17] by regional headquarters in New York and Budapest.

始于1981年离婚后，1983年他与苏珊·威柏（一位比他年轻25岁的艺术史学家）结婚，他们育有两个儿子，在曼哈顿、纽约的长岛、贝德福和伦敦都有家。

2. 主要贡献

索罗斯将其三分之二的时间和年收入的一半用于推动国外的民主及将美国变成更加宽容的社会。1992年，索罗斯捐助1亿美元支持俄罗斯和前苏联的科学家和科学研究，他捐助的目的是希望缓解因苏联解体而产生的"人才流失"，并期望起到像美国国家科学基金一样的作用。同样在1992年，索罗斯给波斯尼亚人民捐款5,000万美元以减轻他们的痛苦。索罗斯现在18个中、东欧国家设立了基金以支持那里的教育、文化和经济活动。他还为匈牙利、波兰和苏联学生设立了牛津奖学金。在世界范围内，他的慈善活动在1997年共雇用了24个国家的1,300余人，这些活动由设立在纽约和布达佩斯的两个地区总部协调管理。

---

[17] coordinate [kəuˈɔːdinit] v.（使）成为同等，（使）协调

In 1993 he was the highest-paid executive on Wall Street , earning $1.1 billion or more. For years he has been a hugely successful money manager and investor, but the $1 billion that he reportedly made in just a few days…by betting against the British pound has turned him into a guru[18]—and his investments are mimicked[19] across the world . He is, however, not immune to failures: George Soros lost $600 million on Feb. 14 when the yen took a jump he had bet against, Soros' Quantum Group said the loss took almost 5% of the fund group's $12 billion in assets. However, $10,000 invested in Soros's Quantum Fund in 1969 was worth more than $21 million in 1994 . By1996 the assets of Soros Fund Management were approximately $15 billion.

Soros is an active author. In 1987 Soros published a book on his financial philosophies titled *The Alchemy of Finance*. In this book he explains his "theory of reflexivity"[20], which is based on his belief that stock prices are not based on facts but in the attitudes of investors.

3. Evaluation

According to *Institutional Investor* Magazine, George Soros is "The world's Greatest Money Manager". Soros also has his share of critics of his approach to both money management and

1993年，索罗斯是华尔街报酬最高的管理人员，其年收入为11亿美元甚至更多。多年来，他都是极其成功的资金管理者和投资者，赌英镑和美元的汇率据说使他在几天之内赚了10亿美元，他成了人人崇拜的权威，他的投资方法被全世界的人模仿。可是，他并不能免于失败，1994年2月14日当日元大幅贬值时，乔治·索罗斯在这一天就损失了6亿美元，索罗斯的量子集团称这一损失使集团120亿美元的资产损失了5%。可是，1969年投资1万美元于索罗斯的量子基金到1994年价值已达2,100万美元，到1996年，索罗斯基金管理公司的资产约为150亿美元。

索罗斯是一位活跃的作家，1987年，索罗斯出版了一本关于他的金融哲学的著作——《金融冶金术》，在这本书中，他解释了他的"反射理论"，他认为股价的高低并不取决于事实而是取决于投资者对它的态度。

3.评价

《机构投资者》杂志说，乔治·索罗斯是世界上最伟大的资金管理人。但也有人批评索罗斯的资金管理和慈善方式，有人认为索罗

---

[18] guru ['guru:] *n.*（受下属崇敬的）领袖，头头
[19] mimic ['mimik] *v.*模仿；模拟
[20] reflexivity [ˌriːflek'sivəti] *n.* 反射

philanthropy. There are some who claim that there is a conflict of interest when Soros invests in countries where he is giving money. In terms of his philanthropy, some say it is too impulsive and mercurial[21] too arrogant and micromanaged. According to Shawcross, "Soros deliberately courts controversy[22] and publicity, trying to build a platform from which to propagate[23] his views".

斯向他投资的国家捐款的时候存在着利益上的冲突。关于他的慈善行为，有人认为太冲动、太多变、太自负，管理太细。据肖克洛斯称，"索罗斯是有意引起争论和提高知名度，以此来建立一个宣传他观点的平台"。

非常点拨

1. Budapest，匈牙利首都，多瑙河将城市一分为二，河西岸称为布达（Buda），东岸称为佩斯（Pest）。布达佩斯人称东欧的巴黎和多瑙河上的明珠，被联合国教科文组织列为珍贵的世界遗产之一，曾经被法国人评为世界上最安静的首都。

2. the International League for Human Rights，国际人权联盟，1991年成立于美国纽约，为国际非政府组织。在联合国，联合国教育、科学及文化组织，国际劳工组织，美洲国家组织，欧洲理事会享有咨商地位。

3. brain drain，人才外流。Brain drain这个说法是在第二次世界大战以后出现的。当时有好多国家的学生，为了学习美国的科学技术，都纷纷到美国的大学来念书。可是，好多学生毕业以后就留在美国了，因为他们在美国工作所得到的工资要比回到自己国家要高。Brain drain就是指一个国家受过高等教育的人才，被别的国家更好的就业机会或者其他条件所吸引而移居国外了。

---

[21] mercurial [mə'kjuəriəl] *a.*活泼的，易变的
[22] controversy ['kɔntrəvə:si] *n.*争论，争吵
[23] propagate ['prɔpəgeit] *n.*传播，宣传；普及

4. Quantum Fund，量子基金，是全球著名的大规模对冲基金，美国金融家乔治·索罗斯旗下经营的五个对冲基金之一。量子基金是高风险基金，主要在世界范围内投资于股票、债券、外汇和商品。量子美元基金在美国证券交易委员会登记注册，它主要采取私募方式筹集资金。据说，索罗斯为之取名"量子"，是源于索罗斯所赞赏的一位德国物理学家、量子力学的创始人海森堡提出的"测不准定理"。索罗斯认为，就像微粒子的物理量子不可能具有确定数值一样，证券市场也经常处在一种不确定状态，很难去精确度量和估计。量子基金（Quantum Fund）和配额基金（Quota Fund）都属于对冲基金(Hedge Fund)。其中，前者的杠杆操作倍数为八倍、后者可达20倍，意味着后者的报酬率会比前者高，但投资风险也比前者大，根据Micropal的资料，量子基金的风险波动值为6.54，而配额基金则高达14.08。

5. *The Alchemy of Finance*，《金融冶金术》，本书是索罗斯的投资日记。读者可以从中欣赏到索罗斯如何分析个股，如何把握市场转变的时机，如何面对不利的市场行情并及时调整对策，从而在风云变幻的金融市场中立于不败之地的精彩艺术。《金融冶金术》是自《股票操盘手回忆录》之后又一部具有永恒价值的投资指南。只有索罗斯才能对如此复杂的事态作出如此透彻的分析。

William D.Gann

Unit 7

William D.Gann
20世纪著名投资家：威廉·江恩

主题札记

　　威廉·江恩（William D.Gann）——20世纪最著名的投资家之一。江恩全名是William Delbert Gann，1878年6月15日生于美国得州小镇Lufkin。少年时代的江恩在火车上卖报纸和送电报，还贩卖明信片、食品和小饰物等。江恩被世人所津津乐道的辉煌事迹是1909年他在25个交易日里赚了本金的10倍！这一年再婚的江恩接受当时著名的《股票行情与投资文摘》杂志访问，在杂志编辑的监督下，江恩在25个交易日里进行了286次交易，其中264次获利，其余22次亏损，胜率高达92.3%，而资本则增值了10倍，平均交易间隔是20分钟。在华尔街投机生涯中，江恩大约赚取了5,000万美元的利润，在今天，相当于5亿美元以上的数量。虽然和其他的一些投资大师相比，他的财富数量并不算什么，但最重要的是他靠自己的新发现去赚取他应得的财富……

阅读长廊

The Remarkable W.D. Gann

杰出的投资家：
威廉·江恩

If you had been a businessman traveling across Texas in 1891, you might have bought a newspaper and a couple of cigars from a tall, lanky[1] 13-year-old selling them on your train. And as you talked with your fellow travelers about investments, you might have noticed the youth eavesdropping[2] intently on your conversation.

If you had asked him, the boy might have told you his name was Willy and, yes, he was interested in commodities. His dad was a farmer in Angelina County, and just about everyone he knew was as well. They were all concerned about the price their cotton would bring. And had you inquired whether young Willy also wanted to till the East Texas soil when he got older, he might have said no, he didn't think so:

　　假如你是一位商人，正好在1891年时穿过得克萨斯州旅行，在火车上你也许会从一个瘦高的13岁男孩那里买过一份报纸和几支烟。当你和其他旅客谈论有关投资的事情时，你可能会留意到那位年轻人正专注地偷听你们的谈话。

　　若你问他，他可能会告诉你他的名字叫威利，是的，他对商品很感兴趣。他的父亲是安格里纳县的一个农民，他认识的每一个人都是农民。他们对于他们的棉花能卖多少价钱很感兴趣。如果你问小威利长大了是否也愿意在得克萨斯东部地区耕作，他也许会说"不"。他并不这么认为，他想当个商人。"那么，祝你好运，小威利！"你

---

[1] lanky ['læŋki] a.过分瘦长的，瘦长得难看的
[2] eavesdrop [i:vz'drɔp] v.偷听

he wanted to be a businessman. "Well, good luck, young Willy," you might have said. "Maybe you'll have your own business some day, maybe you'll even be famous. Who knows? No one can predict the future." The young eavesdropper going up and down the aisles of that train was William Delbert Gann. Was it really true, he might have wondered, that no one can predict the future?

W. D. Gann was born on a farm some seven miles outside of Lufkin, Texas, on June 6, 1878. He was the firstborn of 11 children of Sam Houston Gann and Susan R. Gann. The Ganns lived in a too small house with no indoor plumbing[3] and with not much of anything else. They were poor, and young Willy walked the seven miles into Lufkin for three years to go to school.

But the work he could do on the farm was more important to the family, so W. D. never even graduated from grammar school or attended high school. As the eldest boy, he had a special responsibility, and those years working on the farm may have been the beginning of his lifelong dedication to hard work. His religious upbringing as a Baptist[4] may also have had something to do with it, for his faith stayed with him throughout his life as well.

可能会说，"也许有一天你会有你自己的生意，甚至你会很有名。谁知道呢？没人能预知未来。"这个在火车上走前走后的年轻偷听者就是威廉·德尔伯特·江恩。这是真的吗？他可能想：真的没有人能预知未来吗？

1878年6月6日，江恩出生于距离得克萨斯州路芙根市约7英里的一个农场。他是萨姆·休斯顿·江恩和苏珊·江恩家11个孩子中的老大。江恩家房子太小，甚至没有室内的水管，其他也没有什么东西。他们很穷，有三年时间小威利每天都要走7英里去上学。

但是对于他们家来说，他在农场能做的事情更重要，因此他甚至没有从文法学校毕业，也未曾上过高中。作为家中长子，他有特殊的责任，那些年在农场干活的经历也许是他一生献身艰苦工作的开始。作为一个"浸礼会"教友，宗教培养对他可能有所影响，因为他的信仰伴随着他的一生。

---

[3] plumbing ['plʌmiŋ] *n.*建筑物内的水管装置
[4] Baptist ['bæptist] *n.*（基督教新教）浸礼会教友

A few years later W.D. worked in a broker-age in Texas and attended business school at night. He married Rena May Smith, and two daughters, Macie and Nora, were born in the first few years of the new twentieth century. W.D. made the fateful move to New York City in 1903 at the age of 25.

Working most likely at a major Wall Street brokerage, W.D. made other changes in his life as well. He divorced his Texas bride and in 1908 at the age of 30 married a 19-year-old colleen[5] named Sarah Hannify. W.D. and Sadie had two children—Velma, born in 1909 and W.D.'s only son, John, who arrived six years later. In addition, Macie and Nora came to live with their father and were raised in New York by their Irish stepmother.

During the First World War the family moved from Manhattan to Brooklyn first to Bay Ridge, then to Flatbush. W. D. reportedly predicted the November 9, 1918 abdication[6] of the Kaiser and the end of the war. But it was after the armistice[7] that the fortunes of the Ganns of Brooklyn took their most dramatic turn. The W. D. that traders know today emerged in the Roaring Twenties.

几年以后，江恩在得克萨斯州的一个经纪事务所工作，晚上去商业学校读书。他娶了瑞娜·梅·史密斯，他们的两个女儿玛茜和诺拉也在20世纪初的几年里相继出生。江恩1903年25岁时搬到了纽约，这改变了他的命运。

江恩很可能在华尔街一家主要的经纪公司工作，在生活上也发生了一些变化。1908年，30岁的江恩与他的得州妻子离婚，并娶了一位名叫撒拉·哈尼发的19岁爱尔兰少女。江恩和塞迪（撒拉的昵称）生了两个孩子——维玛于1909年出世，而江恩唯一的儿子约翰则在6年后出世。此外，玛茜和诺拉来到纽约，与她们的父亲同住，由她们的爱尔兰继母抚养长大。

第一次世界大战期间，江恩举家从曼哈顿迁到布鲁克林，先是到拜里奇地区，后又到弗莱特布什地区。据报道，江恩预告了1918年11月9日凯撒的退位和战争的结束。但是在停战以后，住在布鲁克林的江恩的命运发生了戏剧性的转变。现代交易商都熟知的那个江恩在喧嚣的20世纪20年代出山了。

---

[5] colleen ['kɔli:n] *n.* （爱尔兰）少女，姑娘
[6] abdication [ˌæbdi'keiʃən] *n.* 退位，让位
[7] armistice ['aːmistis] *n.* 停火，停战

In 1919 at the age of 41, W. D. Gann quit his job and went out on his own. He spent the rest of his life building his own business. He began publishing a daily market letter, *the Supply and Demand Letter*. The letter covered both stocks and commodities and provided its readers with annual forecasts. Forecasting was an activity with which W.D. had become fascinated[8]. The young business prospered, and three years later W.D. Gann became a homeowner, buying a small house on Fenimore Street in his adopted home of Brooklyn. The market letter led to more ambitious publishing. In 1924 W.D.'s first book, *Truth of the Stock Tape*, was published.

A pioneering work on chart reading, it is still regarded by some as the best book ever written on the subject. An individualist and ambitious hard worker, W.D. self-published *Truth of the Stock Tape* through his new Financial Guardian Publishing Company. He personally wrote his own ads to market it and negotiated with bookstores to carry it. *Truth of the Stock Tape* was praised by *The Wall Street Journal* and sold well for years. Some consider it the best of his many books. For a first effort it was a significant accomplishment[9].

His market forecasts during the twenties were reportedly 85 percent accurate. But W.

1919年他41岁时，江恩辞去了工作，并开始自己创业。他把余生都花在了建立自己的生意上。他开始出版一份每日市场通讯——《供需通讯》。这份通讯涵盖了股票和商品的信息，并且为读者提供每年市场走势预测。预测是江恩比较着迷的一项活动。新业务生意日渐兴隆，三年后，江恩拥有了自己的物业，在布鲁克林的菲尼莫街买了一栋小房子。该市场通讯驱使江恩对出版业有了更大的野心。1924年，江恩的第一本著作——《江恩股市定律》出版了。

这本书是图表分析的先驱，该书至今仍被有些人视为图表分析领域中最杰出的作品。江恩是一位个人主义者，充满野心并努力工作的人。江恩通过他自己的"金融监护出版公司"独立出版了《江恩股市定律》一书。他自己写广告去推销，并且与书店磋商销售。《江恩股市定律》得到《华尔街日报》的赞扬，畅销数年。有些人认为这是他写的众多著作中最好的一本。这是第一次尝试，是一个很重要的成就。

他在20世纪20年代公开发表的市场预测中，准确率高达85%。但

8 fascinate ['fæsineit] *vt.* 使着迷，使极感兴趣
9 accomplishment [ə'kɔmpliʃmənt] *n.*完成（任务等）

D. didn't confine[10] his prognostications[11] to prices. It was widely reported he predicted the elections of Wilson and Harding and, indeed, of every president since 1904. At age 49, W. D. Gann wrote what is perhaps his most unusual book, the 1927 *Tunnel Through the Air*. It is a prophetic work of fiction, not a genre every Wall Street analyst dabbles[12] in. But W.D. Gann was one of a kind. The book is perhaps best known for having predicted that attack on the United States by Japan and an air war between the two powers. Though *Tunnel Through the Air* may have had little to offer investors, it was well-publicized and enhanced its author's growing reputation.

W. D. Gann prospered during the Depression, which he predicted would end in 1932. He acquired seats on various commodities exchanges, traded for his own account, wrote *Wall Street Stock Selector* in 1930 and *New Stock Trend Detector* in 1936. He continued making remarkably accurate forecasts as well as some less successful ones like the electoral defeat of FDR. He developed a new interest in investing in Florida real estate. He became a small-scale home-builder in Miami as well as the owner of a block of stores on the Tamiami Trail.

是江恩的"预言"并不仅局限于价格。有广泛报道称他曾预测过威尔逊（Wilson）和哈定（Harding）总统的选举——实际上是1904年以来的每一位总统的选举。江恩于49岁时写了一本可能是最不同寻常的著作——1927年出版的《空中隧道》，这是一本预言小说，虽然这并不是每一位华尔街分析家都爱好的类型，但是江恩是其中的一位。这本书或许是因为预测到了美国遭受日本的袭击及两强间的空战而名噪一时。虽然《空中隧道》一书给投资者提供的信息很有限，但它引起了公众的重视，也使江恩名声大振。

江恩在大萧条时期甚为成功，他成功预言大萧条将在1932年结束，他买下不同商品交易所的会员席位，并为自己的账户做交易。在1930年，他写了《华尔街股票选择器》，1936年，他写了《新股票趋势探测器》。他继续作出令人侧目的准确猜测，但也有不太成功的猜测，例如富兰克林·罗斯福（FDR）会选举失败。他培养起了一项新的兴趣——投资佛罗里达州的房地产。在迈阿密（Miami），他成为了一个小型房地产商，又拥有森迈阿密（Tamiami Trail）的一系列店铺。

---

[10] confine [kən'fain] *vt.* 限制，局限于
[11] prognostication [prɔg,nɔsti'keiʃən] *n.* 预言，预示
[12] dabble ['dæbl] *vt.*涉猎，浅尝，少量投资

He kept his business in New York, relying on his long-time personal secretary. In Miami he continued studying the market, trading, real estate investing, and instructing students. The next year at the age of 65, when most are thinking retirement, W.D. decided he'd get married and did, to a much younger woman.

The post-war years saw Gann start taking it easier. He published *45 Years in Wall Street* in 1949. He sold his business to Joseph Lederer, a fellow student of the market. Around the same time he also separately sold the rights to all his books to Edward Lambert. He continued, however, to study, teach, and trade. He was made an honorary member of the International Mark Twain Society in 1950.

In 1954 he suffered a heart attack. A year later advanced stomach cancer was discovered. The doctors operated, but W. D. Gann failed to recover. He died in June, 1955, at the age of 77. He was buried with his second wife in Green-Wood Cemetery in Brooklyn at a location that looks toward Wall Street. It was a fitting location since he had studied the Street all his adult life.

依靠他的长期私人秘书，他继续经营在纽约的生意。在迈阿密，他继续研究市场、交易及房地产投资，并且教导学生。第二年，在他65岁的时侯，在这个大多数人正计划退休的年龄，江恩决定再婚，而且他真的做到了，新娘是一位比他年轻许多的女子。

第二次世界大战后，江恩开始放松下来。1949年，他出版了《华尔街45年》，并将他的生意售予约瑟·利德瑞——他的一位学生。几乎同时，他分别将他所有著作的版权售予爱德华·兰伯特。但是，他仍然继续学习、教学及做交易。1950年，他成为国际马克·吐温协会的名誉会员。

1954年，江恩心脏病发。一年后，他发现胃癌已到晚期。医生为他动过手术，但江恩并没有恢复过来。1955年6月江恩去世，享年77岁。他和他的第二任妻子同葬于布鲁克林绿林公墓中一块面向华尔街的墓地。这是一个合适的地点，因为江恩成年后一直致力于研究华尔街。

财经宝库

1. *Truth of the Stock Tape*，《江恩股市定律》。江恩以其人生的巨大成功，证明了他所创造的股市投资理论的正确性；在近一个世纪的股票交易中，江恩的股市定律至今仍被奉为金科玉律，成为传世经典。本书是江恩的一本涵盖股票和期货投资的专著。幽默轻松的语言和22幅股市行情图，深入浅出地揭示了股票和期货投资过程中卓有成效的交易方法。

2. *Wall Street Stock Selector*，《华尔街股票选择器》，江恩的一本著作。股票（或期货）投资者需要华尔街式的教育。本书提供的是永不过时的股市真谛。即使在当今的知识经济时代，其中的知识含量也是充足的。

3. *New Stock Trend Detector*，《新股票趋势探测器》。如同透过蛛丝马迹侦察事实真相一样，华尔街的股票侦探更善于发现、判断买卖双方的实力和庄家的意图。因为无论股市如何起落，都是由股票的买入和卖出决定的，都是人的所思所为。既然是人为，就有被测出和调控的可能，毕竟，人的本性是不变的。多年的经验使江恩确信，通过对个股交易规律的研究，可以探测股市运行的趋势。探测股市走势的关键环节是发现交易数据中的潜在信息，并正确地分析、梳理、跟踪和把握这些信息。

4. FDR, Franklin D. Roosevelt，美国第32任总统富兰克林·D. 罗斯福，一直被视为美国历史上最伟大的总统之一，是20世纪美国最受拥戴的总统，也是美国历史上唯一连任4届总统的人，从1933年3月起，直到1945年4月去世为止，任职长达12年。曾赢得美国民众长达7周的高支持率，创下历史纪录。

富兰克林·D. 罗斯福

5. *45 Years in Wall Street*，《华尔街45年》，江恩著。本书是传奇式的证券交易巨匠江恩多年来在证券交易中所获得的交易经验和研究心得的总结。该书总结了江恩在其45年证券交易生涯中积累的宝贵经验，对每一位涉足证券市场的人都有着十分重要的借鉴意义。

6. honorary member，名誉会员。

DIY工作室

1. Why is William D. Gann still talked about, written about, and studied avidly many years after his passing?

2. One of Gann's books ,*Truth of the Stock Tape*, was praised by *The Wall Street Journal* and sold well for years. What's the main idea of the book?

归类记忆卡片

外汇储备 foreign exchange reserves
固定汇率 fixed exchange rate
浮动汇率 floating/flexible exchange rate
货币期权 currency option
套利 arbitrage
合约价 exercise price
远期升水 forward premium
多头买升 buying long
空头卖跌 selling short
按市价订购 market order

股票经纪人 stockbroker
国际货币基金组织 the IMF
七国集团 the G-7
监督 surveillance
银行间同业拆借市场 interbank market
可兑换性 convertibility
软通货 soft currency
限制 restriction
交易 transaction
充分需求 adequate demand

听力广场

William Delbert Gann—one of the most successful traders that ever lived

In 1995, 40 years after his passing, William D. Gann is still talked about, written about, and studied avidly[13]. It's an extraordinary testimonial[14] to his work and one that even W.D. couldn't have predicted. Or could he? What lessons might there be in this remarkable[15] man's life?

First is an affirmation[16] of the American Dream. William Delbert Gann of Lufkin, Texas, started with nothing. He and his family had no money, no education, and no prospects. But less than 40-years after overhearing businessmen

威廉·江恩——迄今为止最成功的投资家之一

在江恩逝世四十年后的1995年，人们仍然谈论着他，著书讨论，并潜心研究他。这是对他工作的极大肯定，也许连江恩自己都没有预料到。又或者他能够预料得到？我们可以在这位非凡的人的一生中获得些什么经验和教训呢？

首先，这印证了一个"美国梦"的实现。得州路芙根市的威廉·德尔伯特·江恩白手起家。他和他的家人都没有钱，没有受过教育，没有前景。但是，在偷听到商

---

[13] avidly ['ævidli] ad. 贪心地，热心地
[14] testimonial [testi'məuniəl] n.（对某人的人格、能力、工作态度、资格等的）推荐书、证明书，鉴定书；表扬信
[15] remarkable [ri'mɑːkəbl] a.异常的，引人注目的，不寻常的
[16] affirmation [əfə:'meiʃən] n. 断言，主张，肯定

talk on railroad cars in Texas, W.D. Gann was known around the world.

Second, hard work pays. W. D. Gann rose early, worked late, and approached his business with great energy. Virtually all his education was self-administered. This teacher, writer, and prescient forecaster had a third-grade formal education. But he never stopped reading.

Third, unconventional[17] thinking may have its merits. W.D. was intellectually curious to an extraordinary degree. He was unafraid of unorthodox[18] ideas, whether in finance or in other areas of life. He wasn't always right— none of us are—but he dared to pursue a better idea.

Fourth, there may be something to that clean living business after all. A conservative Baptist, W.D. didn't smoke, drink, play cards, or dance. He was serious in demeanor[19] and a conservative dresser, although he lightened up somewhat in his later years. He respected the value of a dollar and was prudent[20] in his personal spending. Not every internationally acclaimed seer[21] would

人们在铁路车厢上的谈话后不到四十年的时间里，江恩扬名世界。

第二，天道酬勤。江恩很早起床，工作至很晚，充满干劲处理他的生意。实际上，他所有的教育都是自学而来。作为一名导师，作家和先知的预测家，他只受过小学三年级的正式教育，但他从未停止过读书。

第三，非常规的思考可能有其价值。江恩对知识的好奇心到了超强的地步。他不惧怕非正统的理念，无论在金融领域或是生活的其他方面都是一样。他不能保证经常正确无误，我们没有人能永远正确，但他敢于追求更好的理念。

第四，可能有某些事物影响一盘有活力的生意。作为一位保守的"浸礼会"教友，江恩从不抽烟，不喝酒，不玩牌，也不跳舞。他态度严肃，衣着保守，尽管他在最后几年里，某种程度上较为放松了。他尊重金钱的价值，他在个人开支上十分谨慎。并不是每一位受到国际瞩目的预言家都能够一直在布鲁

---

[17] unconventional [ʌnkənˈvenʃənl] *a.*非常规的，非传统的
[18] unorthodox [ʌnˈɔːθədɔks] *a.* 非正统的，非传统的，非正规的
[19] demeanor [diˈmiːnə] *n.* (美)（正式用语）行为，举止，态度
[20] prudent [ˈpruːdnt] *a.* 审慎的，有先见之明的，判断力强的
[21] seer [siə] *n.*预言家，先知者

continue to live in a modest house in Brooklyn.

Fifth, faith helps. W. D. Gann studied the Bible all his life. It was his Book of Books. His own last book, *The Magic Word*, published in 1950, strongly reflects this devotion.

And finally, the only lesson for traders I will venture to offer is W.D. Gann never stopped studying the market. Even after his forecasts happened, even after he achieved international acclaim. Although he believed in cycles, he also knew that markets are always changing and that decisions must be made based on today's conditions, not yesterday's.

W.D. might have rested on his laurels[22]. But he kept studying and seeking greater understanding. If he couldn't afford to stop, can any trader afford to do so?

克林的一间普通房子里生活。

第五，信仰帮助了他。江恩一生学习《圣经》。这是他的书中的书。他最后一本著作《魔术的字句》在1950年出版，强烈反映出他对信仰的虔诚。

最后，唯一一个我敢于提供给投资者的经验是，江恩从未停止研究市场，即使在他的预言实现之后，即使在他得到国际威望之后。虽然他相信经济周期，但他也知道市场恒变，决策必须以今天的状况为基础，而并非昨天的。

江恩可能已在成功之上，但他坚持研究，追求更高的境界。连他都孜孜不倦，别的投资者又有什么理由懈怠呢？

---

22 laurel ['lɔrəl] *n.* （表示荣誉的）桂冠，殊荣

非常点拨

1. *The Magic Word*，《魔术的字句》，江恩的最后一本著作，在1950年出版，强烈反映出他对信仰的虔诚。

Benjamin Graham

Unit 8

Benjamin Graham

证券分析之父：本杰明·格雷厄姆

主题札记

　　本杰明·格雷厄姆（Benjamin Graham,1894—1976）——被誉为证券分析之父、华尔街院长。股市向来被视为精英聚集之地，华尔街则是衡量一个人智慧与胆识的决定性场所。本杰明·格雷厄姆作为一代宗师，他的金融分析学说和思想在投资领域产生了极为巨大的震动，影响了几乎三代重要的投资者，如今活跃在华尔街的数十位资产上亿的投资管理人都自称为格雷厄姆的信徒，他享有"华尔街教父"的美誉。

阅读长廊

Who was Benjamin Graham, and why is he worth listening to?

Graham was not just one of the best investors of all time; he remains far and away the greatest thinker about investing who ever lived. As a money manager and a finance professor at Columbia Business School, Graham was a teacher, mentor and hero to such investing giants as Sir John Templeton, William Ruane of the Sequoia Fund, and Charles Munger and Warren Buffett of Berkshire Hathaway. Buffett has said: "Ben had more influence on me than any person except my father···Graham was the smartest man I ever knew."

Graham's text *Security Analysis*, first published in 1934, was the first book to apply rigorous[1] logic and objective standards to the study of stock and bond values. And *The Intelligent Investor*—first published in 1949,

本杰明·格雷厄姆是谁，为什么他值得倾听？

格雷厄姆不仅仅是迄今为止最伟大的投资者之一，他无疑是投资领域最伟大的思想家。作为一个短期资本经营者和哥伦比亚商学院的金融学教授，对于一些投资巨头来说，他更是一位良师益友甚至英雄。如约翰·邓普顿，红杉基金的威廉·洛恩，伯克希尔哈撒韦公司的查尔斯·芒格和沃伦·巴菲特。巴菲特曾经说过："本比除了我父亲之外的任何人对我的影响都大……格雷厄姆是我所认识的人中最聪明的一个。"

格雷厄姆于1934年首次出版了《证券分析》，这是将严谨的逻辑和客观的标准应用于股票和债券研究的第一本书。1949年，他又出版了《聪明的投资者》，格雷厄姆在

---

[1] rigorous ['rigərəs] *a.* 严密的，缜密的

revised four times during Graham's lifetime and again, by Jason Zweig, in 2003 — was the first book that ever explained, for retail[2] investors, the intellectual framework and emotional discipline that are essential for financial success.

What accounts for Graham's influence and innovation? Put simply, by any measure he was one of the most brilliant men of the 20th century. Graham's genius manifested itself on at least five fronts:

- as an intellectual
- as a financier
- as a psychologist
- as an historian
- as a writer

As an intellectual, Graham graduated second in his class at Columbia and, before the end of his senior year, was offered faculty positions in three different departments: English, Greek and Latin, and mathematics. (He was all of 20 years old.) Later, Graham came up with several of the key ideas behind the Bretton Woods agreement that modernized the global financial system. He also patented[3] an improved slide rule, wrote a Broadway play and taught himself Spanish so he could translate a major Uruguayan[4] novel, Mario Benedetti's *The Truce*, into English. (By

有生之年对其进行了4次修订，后来杰森·茨威格在2003年进行了再次修订。这本书首次向普通投资者介绍了获得金融成功所必须拥有的知识框架和情感纪律。

用什么才能解释格雷厄姆的影响和创新？简单来讲，无论用哪种标准，他都是20世纪最聪明的人之一。格雷厄姆的天才至少体现在五个方面：

- 作为一个智者
- 作为一个金融家
- 作为一个心理学家
- 作为一个历史学家
- 作为一个作家

作为一个智者，格雷厄姆在哥伦比亚大学是以全班第二名的身份毕业的。在大学四年级结束之前，他在三个不同的系科拥有教职：英语系、希腊和拉丁语系和数学系。（当时，他只有20岁。）后来，格雷厄姆就布雷顿森林协定提出一些重要观点，而这个协定革新了全球金融体系。他还改进了计算尺并获得专利，编写百老汇剧本，自学西班牙语，并将马里奥·贝内蒂撰写的乌拉圭的一篇重要小说《休战》翻译成英语（在他辞世时，格

---

[2] retail [ri:'teil] *a.*零售的，零售商品的
[3] patent ['peitənt] *vt.* 获得……专利，给予……专利权
[4] Uruguayan [juərə'gwaiən] *a.* 乌拉圭的

the end of his life, Graham knew at least seven languages.) But Graham was not just smart: he was wise.

As a financier, Graham amassed[5] one of the best track records in the history of investing, outperforming the Standard & Poor's 500-stock index by at least 2.5 percentage points annually for a period of more than 20 years. Graham survived the Great Crash of 1929 and, for the rest of his career, issued timely warnings about overvalued markets (including the severe collapse in 1973–1974). He also helped restructure[6] GEICO Corp. and was a fearless advocate for better corporate governance, going so far as to take on the Rockefeller family by shaking up their sheltered interest in the Northern Pipe Line Co..

As a psychologist, Graham cast a bright spotlight on human behavior, revealing subtleties and contradictions that anticipated the findings of Nobel Laureate[7] Daniel Kahneman. Throughout his writings, Graham is not concerned with how people ought to act; instead, he focuses on how they actually behave in the real world. All his recommendations are based not just on what people should do, but on what they can do. Graham knew that self-control and self-

雷厄姆至少精通七种语言）。格雷厄姆不仅仅是聪明，而且富于智慧。

作为一个金融家，格雷厄姆拥有投资领域历史上最好的记录，在20多年中，他每年的表现都至少领先标准普尔500指数2.5个百分点。格雷厄姆在1929年大崩盘中幸存下来，在日后的职业生涯中，他及时地对被高估的市场（包括1973—1974年后的严重股灾）提出警告。他还帮助重组了政府员工保险公司，毫无畏惧地宣扬更好的法人管理，更有甚者，他还参与洛克菲勒家族企业，揭露他们在北方石油管道公司隐藏的利益。

作为一个心理学家，人类行为在格雷厄姆这里一览无余。他揭示了人类心理的细微之处和矛盾，预示了诺贝尔奖得主丹尼尔·卡恩曼后来的发现。综观他的著作，格雷厄姆不关注人类应当怎样行动；相反，他专注于人们在真实的世界中该怎样行动。他的所有建议不仅是基于人们应当做什么，而是他们能够做什么。格雷厄姆明白，自我控制和自学是成功投资的关键。

---

[5] amass [ə'mæs] *vt.* 积累，积聚
[6] restructure [ˌriː'strʌktʃə] *vt.* 重建，改组，重组
[7] Laureate ['lɔːriit] *n.* 资金（荣誉）获得者

knowledge are the keys to successful investing. In his words, "The investor's chief problem—and even his worst enemy—is likely to be himself". If you read nothing but Chapters 1, 8, and 20 of *The Intelligent Investor*, you can get off the self-destructive path that sends so many people astray[8] in their financial lives.

As a historian, Graham had a mastery of the facts about everything and everyone that had come before him. The razor of his logic, sharpened by repeated readings of Aristotle and Plato, made mincemeat[9] out of contemporaries[10] who argued that "valuations[11] don't matter" or that "you can't overpay for a great stock". History taught Graham that the financial markets obey fundamental laws as irrevocable[12] as Newton's laws of thermodynamics[13]. Throughout his books, Graham shows that regression[14] to the mean—what goes up must come down, and what goes way up must come down even harder — is the first law of financial physics. Graham's commanding knowledge of history made him a formidable prophet, since the best way to predict the financial future is simply to understand the past. To avoid

用他的话来讲，"投资者的主要问题——甚至是他的劲敌——可能是他自己"。如果你仅仅阅读《聪明的投资者》的第一章、第八章和第二十章，你就能离开自我毁灭的道路，而这条道路使得许多人在他们的金融生涯中误入歧途。

作为一个历史学家，格雷厄姆掌握了他先前所有人和所有事的情况。他逻辑的锋芒，由于反复阅读亚里士多德和柏拉图的著作而变得犀利，彻底击溃了那些叫嚷着"估价并不重要"或"你不可能为一只股票多付钱"的同时期学者。历史告诉格雷厄姆，金融市场遵循基本法则，这个法则如同牛顿的力学法则一样无法逆转。在其所有著作中，格雷厄姆展示了退回中位理论——涨上去的，还会跌下来；涨得越狠，跌得也就越厉害——这是金融物理学的第一法则。格雷厄姆广博的历史知识使得他成为一位可怕的预言家，因为预测金融未来的最好办法就是简单地理解过去。为避免2000—2002年熊市中的灾难性亏损，你需要做的仅仅是阅读并理解格雷厄姆关于过去泡沫的警告。

---

8 astray [əs'trei] *ad.*迷途，入歧途
9 mincemeat ['mins,mi:t] *n.* 剁碎的肉，肉馅；（喻）彻底击溃；把……驳得体无完肤
10 contemporary [kən'tempərəri] *n.* 同代人，同龄人
11 valuation [ˌvælju'eiʃən] *n.* 估价，估定的价值
12 irrevocable [i'revəkəbl] *a.* 不可改变的，不可反转的
13 thermodynamics ['θə:məudai'næmiks] *n.*[复]（用做单）热力学
14 regression [ri'greʃən] *n.*衰退

disastrous losses in the 2000–2002 bear market, you needed only to have read and understood Graham's warnings about past bubbles. And there's no better way to brace yourself against the booms and busts of the future than by learning what Graham has to say.

As a writer, Graham was a master of formal but clear and classic prose. Large parts of *The Intelligent Investor* are set up as compare-and-contrast exercises. The distinctions that Graham draws between stocks and companies, price and value, investment and speculation, "projection" and "protection", show how to think about the big picture. And his pairing of stocks—one glamorous[15] and overpriced, the other stodgy[16] and cheap—show how to analyze individual investments. Finally, Graham's imaginative brilliance shines forth in his metaphor of "Mr. Market", the manic-depressive neighbor who remains the single best image ever devised for explaining how the stock market really works.

Although Graham was born in 1894 and died in 1976, the proofs continue to pile up with the passage of the years: Graham was not just the greatest investing mind of his time, but he remains the greatest investing mind of all time. Every investor, no matter how much or little you know, can benefit from Graham's ideas and

面对未来的繁荣或失败，没有什么比学习格雷厄姆的话语更有效的振作你自己的方法了。

作为一个作家，格雷厄姆是正式、清朗和古典散文的大家。《聪明的投资者》的大部分内容是以比较和对照的方式来撰写的。格雷厄姆在股票和公司、价格和价值、投资和投机、"预测"和"保护"之间作出区分，显示如何从宏观的角度思考问题。他的两本股票书籍———一本引人入胜，价格昂贵；一本晦涩难懂，价格低廉———展示了如何分析个体投资。最后，格雷厄姆富有想象力的辉煌体现在他的"市场先生"这个比喻上，这是他为了诠释股票市场如何真正运作方面而设计的一个狂躁抑郁的邻居所保持的唯一最好的形象。

尽管格雷厄姆生于1894年，卒于1976年，但随着时间的流逝，不断涌现的材料证明：格雷厄姆不仅是他那个时代最伟大的投资家，而且是亘古至今最伟大的投资家。每个投资者，不管你知识渊博或浅陋，都会从格雷厄姆的思想和沃伦·巴菲特认定的"迄今为止最好

---

[15] glamorous ['glæmərəs] *a.* 富有魅力的，迷人的
[16] stodgy ['stɔdʒi] *a.* 滞涩的，古板的，枯燥无味的

from what Warren Buffett calls "the best book about investing ever written". | 的投资书籍"中获益。

财经宝库

1. money manager，短期资本经营者。

2. John Templeton，约翰·邓普顿，全球投资之父，史上最成功的基金经理之一。邓普顿爵士是邓普顿集团的创始人,一直被誉为全球最具智慧以及最受尊崇的投资者之一。福布斯资本家杂志称他为"全球投资之父"及"历史上最成功的基金经理之一"。2006年，他被美国《纽约时报》评选为"20世纪全球十大顶尖基金经理人"。

3. *Security Analysis*，《证券分析》，本书在长达70年的时间里共发行了5版，计有百万册，充当了无数美国最杰出投资家的启蒙教程，加上本杰明·格雷厄姆与戴维·多德两人在华尔街创下的不朽业绩，《证券分析》一书成为投资方面有史以来最有影响力的著作。它从1934年问世以来，至今仍是人们最为关注的书籍，被誉为投资者的《圣经》。

约翰·邓普顿

DIY工作室

1. Who is "Mr. Market" according to Benjamin Graham?

2. What accounts for Graham's influence and innovation?

归类记忆卡片

短期外债 short-term external debt	资产 assets
汇率机制 exchange rate regime	国际收支 balance of payments
直接标价 direct quotes	贸易差额 balance of trade
资本流动性 capital liquidity	繁荣 boom
普通股 common stock	债券 bond
本国货币 domestic currency	资本 capital
外汇交易市场 foreign exchange market	资本支出 capital expenditures
国际储备 international reserve	商品 commodities
利率 interest rate	商品交易所 commodity exchange
货币贬值 currency devaluation	商品期货合同 commodity futures contract

听力广场

Fools fight for favour in the court of Mr. Market

傻瓜在市场先生面前争风吃醋

People in the City talk of "the view of the market" and "what the market thinks". Of

伦敦金融城里的人喜欢说"市场观点"和"市场认为"。市场当

course, the market does not think; only people think. But the anthropomorphic[17] metaphor[18], which personalises market opinion, influences behaviour. Benjamin Graham, doyen[19] of the value investor, once wrote of the capricious[20], volatile[21] "Mr. Market". Warren Buffett, Graham's successor today, continues this fancy[22].

A different metaphor is common among students of finance. The market is a voting machine, which allows participants to record their diverse views. The market price is a continuously varying record of the average of informed opinions.

While these two modes of description are not completely contradictory[23], their implications differ. The anthropomorphic metaphor is hierarchical[24]. "We might ask the market," City folk will say, but only if they occupy very senior positions or are leading specialists in their field. Such individuals are privileged by direct access to Mr. Market himself. The most discreetly[25] influential figures in the City and on Wall Street

然不会"认为",只有人才会"认为"。但这种将市场拟人化的修辞手法却影响着人们的行为。价值投资者的鼻祖本杰明·格雷厄姆曾写到过这位反复无常、变化多端的"市场先生",他的衣钵传人沃伦·巴菲特继承了这种偏好。

金融系学生有另一个常见的比喻：市场是一个投票机，参与者可以借此记录下各自不同的看法。市场价格就是基于信息形成的各种观点持续变化的记录。

虽然上述两种描述模式并不完全矛盾，但它们的含义是不同的。拟人化的说法是分等级的。"我们或许可以问问市场，"金融城里的人会这么说，但前提是他们职位很高，或者是所在领域的一流专家。这些人的特权来自能够直接接触到"市场先生"。金融城和华尔街最谨慎的权势人物展示了"市场先生"追随者的风格和怪癖。

---

[17] anthropomorphic [ˌænθrəpəˈmɔːfik] *a.* 拟人的

[18] metaphor [ˈmetəfə] *n.* 隐喻

[19] doyen [ˈdɔiən] *n.* (一个团体中的)老前辈，资格最老者，地位最高的人

[20] capricious [kəˈpriʃəs] *a.* 无定见的，变幻莫测的

[21] volatile [ˈvɔlətail] *a.* 易变的，反复无常的，易激动的

[22] fancy [ˈfænsi] *n.* 爱好

[23] contradictory [kɔntrəˈdiktəri] *a.* 矛盾的，抵触的

[24] hierarchical [ˌhaiəˈrɑːkikəl] *a.* 分等级的

[25] discreetly [disˈkriːtli] *ad.* 谨慎地，小心地

display the style and mannerisms[26] of Mr. Market's courtiers[27].

The voting metaphor is democratic. Everyone's opinion counts[28] although some opinions count for more than others. Views are weighted by the amount of money behind them.

For those who think of the market as a person, investment skill is understanding Mr. Market's psychology and anticipating, a little faster than others, his changing moods. Those who think of the market as opinion poll take a skeptical[29] view of all investment skill: they believe that the result of the continuous referendum[30] reflects collective wisdom. Everything that can be known is already in the price of securities. The voting machine metaphor underpins[31] the efficient market hypothesis[32].

Both metaphors are instructive but neither is adequate to describe the world: to take either too seriously leads to error. The voting mechanism metaphor is indispensable[33] to the interpretation of short-term responses. Market

投票机的比喻属于民主范畴。每个人的观点都很重要，不过一些人的观点比其他人更重要。观点的重要程度取决于他们背后的钞票数量。

对于那些将市场看做人的投资者来说，投资技巧就是了解"市场先生"的心理，比别人稍微快一些预见到他情绪的变化。而将市场看做投票机的人则对一切投资技巧都持怀疑态度：他们相信，持续全民投票的结果反映的是集体智慧。所有可知因素都已体现在证券价格之中。投票机的说法支持有效市场的假设。

两种说法都有指导意义，但哪一种都不足以描述全貌，太过刻板地坚持其中一种都会导致错误。投票机制的比喻对于解释短期市场反应是必不可少的。市场参与者投

---

[26] mannerism ['mænərizəm] *n.* （绘画、写作中）过分的独特风格
[27] courtier ['kɔːtjə] *n.* 奉承者，拍马屁的人
[28] count [kaunt] *vi.* 有价值，有重要意义
[29] skeptical ['skeptikəl] *a.* 怀疑性的，好怀疑的
[30] referendum [ˌrefə'rəndəm] *n.* （就某政治问题的）公民投票
[31] underpin [ˌʌndə'pin] *vt.* 为（论据、主张等）打下基础，加强，巩固
[32] hypothesis [hai'pɔθisis] *n.* 假设，假说，前提
[33] indispensable [indis'pensəbl] *a.* 必不可少的，必需的

players vote their expectations of variables for which the range of outcomes, and the process by which the outcomes are revealed, are well defined. The market price reflects an average of prevailing[34] opinions about events such as interest rate decisions and corporate earnings announcements, and market reaction will reflect the difference between that average and the outcome.

But the anthropomorphic metaphor helps explain longer-term trends. The uniformity[35] of conventional wisdom determines the fads[36] and fashions that routinely grip[37] markets. Abrupt changes in the opinion of Mr. Market are the only means of explaining extreme market movements such as the crash of October 1987.

But since there is no Mr. Market, those who chase him pursue their own shadows. In this imagined world, there are no criteria of truth other than what is generally believed to be true. So, as during the New Economy bubble, common belief can become divorced from objective reality. The (first) Gulf war, Jean Baudrillard said, took place only on television. The New Economy, in much the same sense, was observed only on Wall Street. Today, the

票表达他们对各种变量的预期，而他们预期结果的范围以及揭示结果的过程都是有明确定义的。市场价格反映了对利率决策和企业业绩公告等事件的普遍看法的均值，市场反应将体现出均值和结果之间的差异。

但拟人化比喻有助于解释长期趋势。传统智慧的一致性决定了日常影响市场的潮流和时尚。"市场先生"观点的突然变化是解释极端市场变动的唯一方式，如1987年10月的市场崩溃。

但由于"市场先生"其实并不存在，那些追随他的人不过是在追随自己的影子。在这个想象出来的世界中，没有真相的评判标准，只有人们普遍相信什么是真的。因此，正如在新经济泡沫期间，普遍信念可能会与客观现实脱节。法国哲学家让·鲍德里亚说，第一次海湾战争只发生在电视上。与此差不多的是，新经济只能在华尔街观察到。如今，有一种观点认为，相比

---

[34] prevailing [pri'veiliŋ] a. 占优势的，主要的，流行的
[35] uniformity [,ju:ni'fɔməti] n. 无差异，无变化
[36] fad [fæd] n. 流行的时尚、爱好、狂热等
[37] grip [grip] v. 掌握，控制

improbable[38] belief that opaque[39] financing arrangements can generate returns far in excess of those earned on underlying investments acquires validity[40] only from being generally believed.

But if the anthropomorphic metaphor is too relativist, the alternative view is too rationalist. The metaphor of market as voting machine gives too much credence[41] to the coherence[42] of collective wisdom. As Mr. Buffett has observed, the efficient market hypothesis is 90 percent true but the difference between 90 percent and 100 percent is night and day.

The pragmatism[43] that judges wisdom by results confirms the investment philosophy of the Sage[44] of Omaha. Mr. Market is a silly old fool who occasionally makes assets available to Berkshire Hathaway below their fundamental value. The voters in the market referendum are overpaid know-it-alls whose opinions count for little relative to the shrewd[45] assessment[46] of the wise observer, who is not swept up in the intrigues of Mr. Market's court.

实实在在的投资，不透明的融资安排能创造多得多的利润——这种观点只是在被普遍认可的情况下才有效。

但如果说拟人化比喻太过相对主义，那么另一个观点则太过理性。将市场比做投票机的说法过于相信集体的智慧。正如巴菲特所观察得出的，有效市场的假设有90%是真实的，但90%和100%之间有着天壤之别。

根据结果评判智慧的实用主义证明了巴菲特这位"奥马哈圣贤"的投资哲学。"市场先生"是个老傻瓜，偶尔会让伯克夏·哈撒韦公司(Berkshire Hathaway)买到低于基本价值的资产。市场公投中的投票者是一些钱拿得过多、自以为无所不知的人，相对于没有被"市场先生"领地上的阴谋扫地出门的精明观察者的精明评估，他们的观点无足轻重。

---

[38] improbable [im'prɔbəbl] a. 不大可能是真实的，不大可能的
[39] opaque [əu'peik] a. 不透明的，难理解的，晦涩的
[40] validity [və'liditi] n. 有效，效力，合法性
[41] credence ['kri:dəns] n.相信，信任
[42] coherence [kəu'hiərəns] n. 条理性，连贯性，一致性
[43] pragmatism ['prægmətizəm] n.（哲）实用主义
[44] sage [seidʒ] n. 圣人，智者
[45] shrewd [ʃru:d] a.机灵的，聪明的
[46] assessment [ə'sesmənt] n. 评价，看法

非常点拨

1. Jean Baudrillard，让·鲍德里亚，法国哲学家，现代社会思想大师，知识的“恐怖主义者”。他在“消费社会理论”和“后现代性的命运”方面卓有建树，在20世纪80年代这个被叫做“后现代”的年代，让·鲍德里亚在某些特定的圈子里，作为最先进的媒介和社会理论家，一直被推崇为新的麦克·卢汉。

Marcel Ospel
Unit 9

Marcel Ospel
瑞银前董事长：马塞尔·奥斯佩尔

主题札记

作为欧洲最大金融集团的掌门人，奥斯佩尔在瑞士金融界驰骋多年，如今却因次贷危机马失前蹄。这个唯一被允许在瑞银总部大楼抽烟的人，究竟怀着怎样的心情，抽完在董事长办公室里的最后一根烟？

在瑞银集团（UBS）董事长办公室待了7年之后，马塞尔·奥斯佩尔（Marcel Ospel）百感交集地抽完最后一根烟，在2008年的4月初黯然离开。这么多年来，他是唯一被允许在瑞银苏黎世总部大楼里抽烟的人。瑞银从一个老牌银行逐渐成长为欧洲最大的金融集团和全球最大的私人银行，奥斯佩尔可谓居功至伟，所以他也当仁不让地居于这个金融帝国的核心地位，并且成为欧洲年薪最高的高管。然而，他也直接或间接地给瑞银带来了有史以来最大的一次伤害——瑞银2008年4月1日的财务报表显示，在过去的9个月内，瑞银已经因次贷危机亏损了400亿美元，成为迄今为止这场危机中银行业最大的输家之一。在众多股东的压力下，自言"已作出了能做的所有贡献"的奥斯佩尔不得不引咎辞职，而这也标志着瑞银一个时代的终结。

阅读长廊

The Inscrutable Banker

Marcel Louis Ospel was born on February 8, 1950 in Basel, Switzerland. He is the former Chairman of the Board of Directors of UBS AG, the largest bank in Switzerland.

When Ospel turned 16, he was given two choices for the next stage of his life: he could continue with his schooling, or he could take a job with a small bank in Basel, Switzerland. He decided to take advantage of Switzerland's apprentice program, in which he worked for the bank for three years while attending school.

His first job in the late 1960s consisted of going every day to the stock exchange, where he learned firsthand about the stock market from the bottom up. He ran around the exchange floor with pieces of paper to aid in his company's arbitration with foreign exchanges. When his three years ended, he went to Geneva and worked in the trading division of a private bank. He decided after a short time that he should attend school, so he went back to Basel and completed a three-

不可思议的银行家

马塞尔·路易斯·奥斯佩尔1950年2月8日出生于瑞士巴塞尔。他是瑞士最大的银行瑞银的已经离任的董事会主席。

奥斯佩尔16岁时，他面临着人生中的第一个重大选择：是继续循规蹈矩坚持学业，还是直接在巴塞尔当地的一家小银行开始工作？他决定利用瑞士学徒项目的有利条件，上学的同时为这家银行工作了三年。

他在20世纪60年代末期的第一份工作包括：每天去证券交易所，从最底层做起，了解证券市场的第一手信息。他在交易所里，拿着能够帮助他们公司决定外汇交易的文件跑来跑去。三年工作结束以后，他跳槽去日内瓦一家私人银行的交易部门工作。不久，他发现他需要重回校园去补充更多的专业知识，于是他返回老家巴塞尔，用三年的时间从当地的一所经济贸易管

year degree at the School of Economics and Business Administration before beginning his career at SBC in 1977.

Interviewing Marcel Ospel, Switzerland's best-known and, until recently, most handsomely paid banker, is like climbing a wall of polished marble.

The head of UBS, Europe's biggest casualty of the US subprime[1] crisis, is invariably[2] polite, friendly and impeccably[3] dressed—a trademark triangular handkerchief protruding[4] from his top pocket. Light refreshments[5] are served and conversation is cordial. Customarily, such meetings take place in an anonymous[6] room at the Zurich headquarters of the world's biggest wealth manager. Occasionally, privileged guests gain access to Mr. Ospel's inner sanctum[7]—a large, light, but surprisingly unrevealing office dominated by a giant model of Alinghi, the UBS-sponsored yacht that has twice won sailing's coveted[8] America's Cup.

The meeting ends with pleasantries all round. Like the perfect Swiss private banker, Mr. Ospel accompanies his visitor to the lift.

理学校获得了一个文凭，之后，他于1977年开始了他在瑞士银行公司的工作。

马塞尔·奥斯佩尔是瑞士最有名的银行家，就在不久以前，他也是该国收入最高的银行家，采访他就像是攀援一堵光滑的大理石墙（你很难从他那里获得有用信息）。

身为瑞银(UBS)——美国次贷危机中欧洲最大的受害者——的董事长，奥斯佩尔总是彬彬有礼、态度友善、衣着得体——标志性的三角丝巾从西服胸袋上露出一角。茶点摆了上来，谈话热情诚恳。通常，此类会见的地点都是这家全球最大财富管理机构苏黎世总部的一个无名房间。偶尔，贵宾也会获准进入奥斯佩尔的内室——一个宽敞、明亮但异常普通的办公室，显眼的位置摆着一艘阿灵基号巨型船模——瑞银赞助的这艘帆船曾两度夺得令人艳羡的美洲杯帆船赛冠军。

会面在轻松愉快的气氛中结束。像标准的瑞士私人银行家一样，奥斯佩尔会将来宾送上电梯。

---

[1] subprime ['sʌb'praim] a. 次要的

[2] invariably [in'veəriəbli] ad. 始终不变地，总是

[3] impeccably [im'pekəbli] ad. 无错误地，极好地，无瑕疵地

[4] protrude [prə'tru:d] vt.&vi. （使某物）伸出，（使某物）突出

[5] refreshment [ri'freʃmənt] n. 茶点，点心

[6] anonymous [ə'nɔniməs] a. 无名的，不具名的

[7] sanctum ['sæŋktəm] n.私室

[8] covet ['kʌvit] v.贪求，觊觎

Only on the way down does the realisation dawn that, stripped[9] of small talk, no information of substance has changed hands. For the rock climber striving for grip, Mr. Ospel's facade[10] offers no handholds.

Inscrutability[11] is the watchword[12] of the 58-year-old chairman of UBS for the past seven years. He is regularly depicted as an ice-cold power broker with an instinctive sense of personal advantage, but ego[13] or guile[14] never mar[15] his public persona[16]. "He's not in any sense the classical banker. That makes him hard to call, which has often worked to his advantage," says Dirk Schütz, editor of the Swiss business magazine Bilanz, who wrote a biography of Mr. Ospel last year.

Behind the public facade, Mr. Ospel is a complex character. Born into a working-class family in Basle, he joined Swiss Bank Corporation at 27 in planning and marketing. An aptitude[17] for trading saw him climb the ladder in capital markets, including stints in London and New York, before moving in 1985 to Merrill

直到电梯下降了，人们才开始意识到，除了闲聊之外，自己什么实质性信息都没有得到。对于努力找地方抓握的攀岩者而言，奥斯佩尔这堵墙连一个握点都没有。

对于担任瑞银董事长已达7年的奥斯佩尔来说，城府深密就是他的座右铭。今年58岁的他常常被描写成一位冷冰冰的权力掮客，天生就有一种个人优越感。但自负和狡诈从来无损于他的公众形象。瑞士商业杂志Bilanz总编德克·舒茨表示："他绝非传统意义上的银行家，因而很难猜到他会怎么出牌，这通常对他有利。"舒茨去年撰写了一部奥斯佩尔的传记。

在公开的外表背后，奥斯佩尔是一位复杂的人物。他出生在巴塞尔的一个工人阶级家庭，27岁时加入了瑞士银行公司（Swiss Bank Corporation）的计划与市场部。交易方面的天资让他在资本市场的阶梯上一路攀升，期间曾被派往伦敦和纽约工作。1985年，他转投美林

---

9 strip [strip] v. 从……中删去不必要的部分

10 facade [fə'sɑːd] n.（建）（房屋的）正面

11 inscrutability [in,skruːtə'biliti] n. 不能预测，不能理解，不可思议

12 watchword ['wɔtʃwəːd] n. 暗语，格言，口号

13 ego ['iːgəu] n. 自我，自己；自负

14 guile [gail] n. 奸猾，狡诈

15 mar [maː] vt. 毁坏，损坏

16 persona [pə'səunə] n. 人格面貌，外表形象

17 aptitude ['æptitjuːd] n.（学习方面的）才能，资质，天质

Lynch, where he helped to expand operations in Zurich.

Two years later, he returned to SBC, rising eventually to chief executive. He took the same post after the bank's 1997 merger with the bigger, Zurich-based Union Bank of Switzerland—to form the UBS of today—before securing the chairmanship in 2001.

He retained a firm grip on power by ensuring himself an executive role. In his 40 years in the business, his pay has risen from SFr110 a month as an apprentice to more than SFr26m (£12.3m) in his best year as boss.

The fierce ambition behind his rise was stoked by his status as an outsider. Mr. Schütz notes: "From early days, he said, 'I wanted to be the boss.' By Swiss standards, especially at the time, that was very unusual—very American."

Unlike many banking peers, Mr. Ospel boasts neither a business nor law degree—nor a doctorate in economics from some hallowed[18] seat of learning. He left school at 17 and took up lowly positions in the stock market departments of Basle banks, before gaining an academic qualification eight years later at a local further education institute.

His private life is low key. Interests include

（Merrill Lynch），帮助美林拓展了在苏黎世的业务。

两年后，他回到瑞士银行公司，最终升任首席执行官。1997年，在该行与规模更大的瑞士联合银行（Union Bank of Switzerland）合并成为今天的瑞银之后，奥斯佩尔仍然担任首席执行官，并在2001年成为公司董事长。

通过确保自己承担管理职责，他保留了对权力的紧密掌控。在40年的职业生涯中，他的工资已经从当学徒时的每月110瑞士法郎，升至当老板的巅峰时期的超过2,600万瑞士法郎。

奥斯佩尔的局外人身份，激发了他追逐升迁的勃勃野心。舒茨指出："从很早的时候，他就在说'我想当老板'。在瑞士人看来，尤其在当时，这很不寻常——非常美国化。"

与银行业的许多同辈不同，奥斯佩尔既没有商科学位，也没有法律学位，更没有知名高等学府的经济学博士头衔。他17岁离开学校，从巴塞尔本地银行股市部门的低层干起，8年之后才从当地一所继续教育学院获得了一个文凭。

奥斯佩尔的私生活相当低调。

---

[18] hallowed ['hæləud] *a.* 神圣化的，神圣的

golf and fast cars (a yellow Ferrari lurks[19] in some garage but is seldom seen). But Mr. Ospel has become slightly more public since his third marriage two years ago to a Zurich entrepreneur and former UBS employee, more than 25 years his junior. The couple celebrated with a lavish[20] bash at the Palace hotel in Gstaad, one of Switzerland's most expensive retreats. Mr. Ospel has a chalet in the exclusive village, a magnet to many of Europe's millionaires.

Although he now spends more time enjoying himself, Mr. Ospel's sense of power and legendary survival skills have not dimmed. It may be too soon to write him off, despite the drubbing[21] he received at the hands of UBS shareholders. A colleague tells of a business trip in which Mr. Ospel was briefed on the bigwigs[22] he was to meet. He was interested only in the connections they had used to climb the ladder. His own ability, late last year, to tap contacts to organize a SFr13bn cash injection from sovereign investors in Singapore and Saudi Arabia helped to shore up his position. The money, he says, was promised "within days".

Conscious of his formidable[23] reputation and

他的个人兴趣包括高尔夫和跑车（一辆黄色法拉利就藏在某个车库里，但人们很少见到）。不过，在两年前与一位比自己小25岁的苏黎世企业家、瑞银前员工喜结连理，第三次步入婚姻殿堂后，奥斯佩尔的公开露面稍微增多了一些。当时，这对夫妇在格施塔德（Gstaad）的王宫大酒店（Palace hotel）大宴宾客，以示庆祝。格施塔德是瑞士最为昂贵的疗养地之一，吸引着许多欧洲富豪。奥斯佩尔在这座世外桃源有一所木屋。

虽然奥斯佩尔现在把更多时间放在了享乐上，但他的权力欲和传奇般的生存技能并未就此黯淡下去。尽管瑞银股东大肆攻击奥斯佩尔，现在就把他一笔勾销或许还为时过早。他的一位同事谈到一次出差经历：在出差途中，员工向奥斯佩尔简要介绍了将要会见的重要人物，他只对这些人在升迁过程中用到的关系感兴趣。去年底，他通过熟人从新加坡和沙特阿拉伯的主权基金获得了130亿瑞士法郎的现金注资——这种利用关系的能力帮助他稳固了自己的地位。他表示，自己"只用了几天"就获得了注资承诺。

人们知道奥斯佩尔令人生畏的

---

[19] lurk [ləːk] *vi.* 潜伏，埋伏，潜在
[20] lavish ['læviʃ] *a.* 过分慷慨的，非常浪费的，太多的
[21] drubbing ['drʌbiŋ] *n.* 殴打，彻底击败
[22] bigwig ['bigwig] *n.* 要人，有重大影响的人
[23] formidable ['fɔːmidəbl] *a.* 可怕的，令人畏惧的；令人惊叹（钦佩）的

his current strains, few will talk about Mr. Ospel publicly. Those willing to comment anonymously invariably focus on his Machiavellian[24] side. Most refer to his role in the abortive[25] 2001 talks to save Swiss-air, Switzerland's cherished national airline. Although the circumstances remain shadowy, many Swiss believe that his absence at a crucial juncture, when financing commitments were essential, was deliberate[26].

Soon after, Mr. Ospel faced down a challenge to his leadership from Luqman Arnold, UBS's British-born chief executive, who accused the chairman of overstepping his powers. After his appeal to UBS's board failed, Mr. Arnold was forced out, leaving Mr. Ospel stronger than ever. "He is very conscious of power and how to use it. You just have to look at the long list of people who've left the bank," says Mr. Schütz.

In another case last summer, Peter Wuffli, a more recent chief executive, departed in similarly strange circumstances. Few swallow the official UBS line that Mr. Ospel wanted to anoint[27] Mr. Wuffli as his eventual successor, but was overruled by fellow board members. Many suspect the truth lies partly in Mr. Ospel's reluctance to make way.

声誉，也了解他目前的压力，很少有人会公开谈论他。那些愿意匿名评论他的人，都把焦点放在了他权谋政治家的一面，无一例外。多数人提到他2001年在中途夭折的拯救瑞士航空（Swiss-air）谈判中扮演的角色。瑞航当时是瑞士所钟爱的国有航空公司。虽然具体情况仍不明朗，但很多瑞士人相信，奥斯佩尔是故意在融资承诺至关重要的时刻缺席的。

此后不久，奥斯佩尔压服了鲁克曼·阿诺德向其领导地位发起的挑战。瑞银的英籍首席执行官阿诺德指责这位董事长越权行事。在向董事会上诉失败后，阿诺德被迫离任，结果，奥斯佩尔的权力比以前更大了。舒茨表示："他很在意权力，而且知道如何运用。你只要看看长长的瑞银离职人员名单就明白了。"

还有一件事情，去年夏季，距今更近的首席执行官胡皓华同样离奇地宣布离职。很少有人相信瑞银的官方说法，即奥斯佩尔想指定胡皓华为自己的最终接班人，但被其他董事会成员否决。很多人猜测，事实真相的一部分就是奥斯佩尔不想让位。

---

[24] Machiavellian [ˌmækiə'veliən] *n.* 权谋政治家
[25] abortive [ə'bɔːtiv] *a.*落空的，失败的
[26] deliberate [di'libəreit] *a.*故意的，蓄意的
[27] anoint [ə'nɔint] *v.* 施以涂油礼

That stubbornness will next be put to the test next month at the group's regular shareholders' meeting, where Mr. Ospel will stand for re-election. Already, he has manoeuvred[28] adroitly[29] to protect his position. Last week, he anticipated reforms in Swiss corporate governance by proposing that UBS board members should in future have only one-year terms instead of their current three-year mandates.

Although Mr. Ospel's re-election is not assured, the fact that he will be seeking only a 12-month extension has improved his chances of success. And, by the next shareholders' meeting in April 2009, who knows where UBS will be?

在下个月瑞银的例行股东大会上，奥斯佩尔的固执将再次受到考验。这次会议将决定他能否再次参加选举。他已经迅速采取了行动来保护自己的地位。上周，他抢在瑞士企业治理改革之前提出建议，未来瑞银董事会成员的任期应该只有1年，而不是目前的3年。

虽然奥斯佩尔的再次当选还没有板上钉钉，但只寻求延长12个月任期的事实，的确提高了他成功的几率。而且，到2009年4月召开下次股东大会时，谁又知道瑞银会变成什么样了呢？

财经宝库

1. 马塞尔·奥斯佩尔的漫画。这是瑞士卢塞恩狂欢节上游行时的马塞尔·奥斯佩尔的漫画像，表示奥斯佩尔在金币中边洗澡，边抽烟。

2. UBS，全称是Union Bank of Switzerland，瑞士联合银行。最初的瑞士大银行有八家，经过多次合并重组，特别是1993年和1997年两次重量级的"大象联姻"

马塞尔·奥斯佩尔的漫画像

---

28 manoeuvre [mə'nu:və] *vt.* 熟练而巧妙地引导
29 adroitly [ə'drɔitli] *ad.* 熟练地，敏捷地

（信贷银行与人民银行、联合银行与银行公司），如今的瑞士大银行仅存瑞士联合银行和瑞士信贷集团两家。

3. Basle，巴塞尔，位于莱茵河湾与德法两国交界处，是连接法国、德国和瑞士的最重要交通枢纽，三个国家的高速公路在此交汇。巴塞尔市内有三个火车站，分别属于法、德、瑞三国；一个跨越瑞法两国国界的国际机场（Basel-Mulhouse airport）和一个莱茵河工业内河港口。

巴塞尔

4. Swiss Bank Corporation，瑞士银行公司，瑞士银行的前身。

5. Ferrari，法拉利，是一家意大利汽车生产商，主要制造一级方程式赛车及高性能跑车，1929年由恩佐·法拉利创办。早期的法拉利赞助赛车手及生产赛车，1946年独立生产汽车，其后变成今日的规模，现在由快意汽车集团拥有，总部设于意大利摩德纳（Modena）附近Maranello。意大利汽车有"二王一后"。二王分别是"法拉利"、"兰博基尼"，一后就是"玛莎拉蒂"。

6. SFr，全称是Swiss Franc，意为瑞士法郎，是瑞士货币单位。

7. Saudi Arabia，沙特阿拉伯，全称是Kingdom of Saudi Arabia。位于阿拉伯半岛；东濒波斯湾，西临红海，同约旦、伊拉克、科威特、阿联酋、阿曼、也门等国接壤。

DIY工作室

1. How to understand the sentence in the text: "He's（Marcel Ospel）not in any sense the classical banker"?

2. Can you explain Mr. Ospel's sense of power and legendary survival skills?

归类记忆卡片

董事会 board of directors	信贷二部 second credit dept
行长 president	质量指标 mass index
经理办公室 executive office	价格通道 price channel
人事部 personnel dept	投射带 projection bands
总务部 general affairs dept	趋势线 trendlines
综合计划部 co-ordination & planning dept	成交量指标 volume
国际业务部 international dept	加权收盘价 weighted close
海外部 overseas branches dept	之字形指标 zigzag
外汇资金部 foreign exchange dept	总卖空比率 total short ratio
信贷一部 first credit dept	相对波动性指标 relative volatility index

听力广场

Marcel Ospel's Management Style

Ospel broke the rules not only in Swiss banking circles but also with his own management style and personal characteristics. While working with Merrill Lynch, he established a

马塞尔·奥斯佩尔的管理风格

奥斯佩尔不仅在瑞士银行界，而且在管理风格和个人特色上也打破了常规。在美林工作时，他就建立了酷似美国投资银行家的管

style resembling that of a US investment banker.

While Ospel loved a nontraditional style of dress and office accoutrements[30], his colleagues sometimes described him as quietly thoughtful. In his first years as CEO of SBC, he was described as a leader who delegated and encouraged his employees. Ospel believed that in a corporation as large as SBC, an autocratic[31], centralized management style would be impossible to maintain. He also said that as the CEO, he was not skilled in every area of the business; therefore, placing key individuals with the proper experience was key to running a company like SBC.

His policy of no dress code at SBC earned the bank and the banker the reputation of having a unique style in the more conservative banking culture. Ospel said that a dress code added nothing to the company except to make employees uncomfortable by requiring them to wear a tie.

However, it was his knowledge of the inner workings of financial markets and an emphasis on strategies and management that received much of the attention in the late 1990s.

When *Euromoney* interviewed him in 1997,

理风格。

虽然奥斯佩尔喜欢非传统的服饰风格和办公装备，他的同事们有时也会认为他比较体贴。在他担任SBC的首席执行官的最初几年里，人们认为他是一个能代表雇员并鼓励雇员的领导。奥斯佩尔相信，在SBC这样一个大公司里，独裁的、中央集权的管理风格是不可能维持的。他还说，作为首席行政官，他不是对公司的所有业务都精通；所以，把有相应经验的重要人物安排到合适的位置对于管理SBC这样的公司是非常重要的。

在日益保守的银行文化中，他不规定SBC职员服装的做法为银行和银行家赢得了声誉，他们的管理风格独一无二。奥斯佩尔说对于服装的规定除了让员工因为不得不带领带觉得不舒服以外，给公司不会带来任何效益。

然而，在20世纪90年代末期，引起人们注意的主要是他的关于金融市场的内部运作的知识和他对策略和管理的重视。

1997年，当《欧洲货币》杂志

---

[30] accoutrements [ə'kutəmənt] *n.*军人的配备，服装
[31] autocratic [,ɔːtə'krætik] *a.*独裁的，专制的

Ospel said he knew that his life would change after the Warburg deal. He had worked hard at analyzing the market before suggesting the merger[32] but had finally determined that the European market looked better in the future than Wall Street. Ospel said in the interview, "So we were primed[33] to do some type of a corporate deal, either in the States or in Europe. I knew that would completely change my professional and personal life. I might have ended up in London or New York. But I'm a mobile person and flexible about these sorts of things"（April 1997）

Despite agreeing to the interview with *Euromoney*, Ospel maintained that bankers should always keep a low public profile, leaving a high-profile lifestyle to the politicians. He also stressed intellectual honesty as the attribute most important to him in an employee, surrounding himself with successful individuals with strong ethics.

By 2000 Ospel had begun losing his reputation as a fair employer and delegator. The press criticized him as being an active president and not clearly defining other positions within the company. He was accused of surrounding himself with people who agreed with him without considering their abilities in international banking.

采访他时，奥斯佩尔说他知道沃伯格交易之后他的生活会有很大的改变。在建议两个公司合并前，他努力分析市场，最后认为在将来欧洲市场看起来要比华尔街好。在那次采访中，奥斯佩尔说："在美国或者欧洲，我们准备好了做一笔合并交易。我知道那将会完全改变我的职业生涯和个人生活。我的事业可能在伦敦或在纽约结束。但是我是一个经常变动住所的人，我对这些事情很能适应。"（1997年4月）

虽然奥斯佩尔同意《欧洲货币》的采访，他始终坚持银行家应该保持低调的公众形象，高调的公众形象应该留给那些政治家。他还强调，知识和诚信是他最看重的雇员的品质，所以他周围有很多有很高道德标准的成功人士。

到2000年，他渐渐失去了他作为一个公平雇主和代表的声誉。媒体批评他作为现任董事长，在公司内部没有明确规定其他职位。他被指责重用一些附和他的人，却并不考虑他们是否有在跨国银行工作的能力。

---

[32] merger ['mə:dʒə] *n.* (两个公司的)合并
[33] prime [praim] *vt.* 使准备好，使完成准备工作

Euroweek painted an unflattering[34] picture of Ospel as a leader who filled positions at UBS with his friends and admirers, reporting that dissension[35] was not allowed, and "when you pass the great man, you no longer say, 'guten morgen, Herr Ospel', but 'Hail Caesar!'" (February 22, 2002).

Industry insiders hinted that Ospel did not enjoy sharing power and that his desire for control led to many of the problems with management from 2000 to 2002.

《欧元周》描述了一个逼真的奥斯佩尔领导形象，他把他的朋友和崇拜者安排在瑞银的各个职位，他不允许有意见分歧，"当你经过那个伟大人物的时候，你不再说'早上好，奥斯佩尔先生'，你会说'万福凯撒！'"（2002年2月22日）

公司内部知情者暗示奥斯佩尔不喜欢跟别人分享权力，他的控制欲导致了从2000年到2002年管理方面的很多问题。

非常点拨

1. Merrill Lynch, 美林公司，其业务涵盖投资银行的所有方面，包括债券及股票的承销（1997年以总融资额2,480亿美元的成绩雄踞全球承销市场之首）、二级市场经纪及自营业务、资产管理、投融资咨询及财务顾问，以及宏观经济、行业、公司的调研。自1988年起，美林连续10年成为全球最大的债券及股票承销商。美林集团在纽约交易所、伦敦交易所和其他许多股票交易市场的股票交易额均名列首位。2008年9月15日，美林公司同意以大约440亿美元的价格将自己出售给美国银行。

2. *Euromoney*，《欧洲货币》，英文杂志月刊，内容主要关于国际银行业及资本市场。

3. Caesar，全名盖尤斯·尤利乌斯·凯撒（公元前102年至公元前44年），古罗马大法官，终身独裁官。

---

[34] unflattering ['ʌn'flætəriŋ] *a.*不奉承的，不恭维的，耿直的，坦率的
[35] dissension [di'senʃən] *n.*意见不合，纠纷，争吵

James D. Wolfensohn

Unit 10

James D. Wolfensohn

世界银行前行长：
詹姆斯·戴维·沃尔芬森

主题札记

　　1995年沃尔芬森被任命为世界银行行长以后，开始着手实现他的愿望。"当我告诉同事们我要去世界银行的时候，我不禁流下了眼泪，"他说，"我想干更伟大的事业，我要把自己的一生贡献给它。"他打算同世界范围内的贫困作斗争。到世界银行工作的决定至今没有令沃尔芬森后悔。詹姆斯·戴维·沃尔芬森在他的一生中实现了很多梦想。他参加过奥运会，通过自身的努力成为百万富翁，在卡内基音乐大厅举办了个人大提琴演奏会，结婚40年来和妻子相濡以沫，3个孩子令他的生活更加美满。

阅读长廊

James D. Wolfensohn: The Former President of the World Bank

James D. Wolfensohn was the World Bank Group's president. Born in Australia in December 1933, he is a naturalized[1] US citizen. He holds a BA and LLB from the University of Sydney and an MBA from the Harvard Graduate School of Business.

Before attending Harvard, he was a lawyer in the Australian law firm of Allen & Hemsley. Mr. Wolfensohn served as an Officer in the Royal Australian Air Force, and was a member of the 1956 Australian Olympic Fencing Team. Mr. Wolfensohn is a Fellow of the American Academy of Arts and Sciences and a Fellow of the American Philosophical Society. He has been the recipient of many awards for his volunteer work, including the first David Rockefeller Prize of the Museum of Modern Art in New York for

世界银行前行长：詹姆斯·戴维·沃尔芬森

詹姆斯·戴维·沃尔芬森曾是世界银行行长。他于1933年12月出生于澳大利亚，现已加入美国籍。他曾获悉尼大学的文学学士和法学学士学位和哈佛大学商学院的工商管理硕士学位。

在上哈佛大学商学院之前，他是澳大利亚爱伦赫姆斯利律师事务所的律师。沃尔芬森先生曾服役于澳大利亚皇家空军，也是1956年澳大利亚奥林匹克击剑队队员。沃尔芬森先生是美国艺术和科学研究院会员和美国哲学学会会员。他从事过许多公益性工作，为此得到许多的嘉奖，其中包括纽约现代艺术博物馆为表彰他在文化艺术领域的工作向他颁发的首届洛克菲勒奖。

---

[1] naturalize ['nætʃərəlaiz] *v.* 使入国籍

his work for culture and the arts.

In May 1995 he was awarded an Honorary Knighthood by Queen Elizabeth II for his contribution to the arts. Mr. Wolfensohn has also been decorated[2] by the Governments of Australia, France, Germany, Morocco, and Norway.

He and his wife, Elaine, an education specialist and a graduate of Wellesley, BA, and Columbia University, MA and MEd, have three children—Sara, Naomi, and Adam.

Before setting up his own company, Mr. Wolfensohn held a series of senior positions in finance. He was Executive Partner of Salomon Brothers in New York and head of its investment banking department. He was Executive Deputy Chairman and Managing Director of Schroders Ltd. in London, President of J. Henry Schroders Banking Corporation in New York, and Managing Director, Darling & Co. of Australia.

Prior[3] to joining the Bank, Mr. Wolfensohn was an international investment banker. His last position was as President and Chief Executive Officer of James D. Wolfensohn Inc., his own investment firm set up in 1981 to advise major US and international corporations. He

1995年5月，为了表彰他对艺术的贡献，英国女皇伊莉莎白二世授予他名誉爵士爵位。沃尔芬森先生也得到过澳大利亚、法国、德国、摩洛哥和挪威政府的授勋。

他与妻子伊莱恩(教育专家，获威斯利大学学士，哥伦比亚大学文学硕士和教育学硕士)育有三个子女——萨拉、内奥米和亚当。

在成立自己的公司之前，沃尔芬森先生在金融界担任过一系列高级职务。他曾经是纽约索罗门兄弟公司的执行合伙人兼投资银行部主任、伦敦施罗德有限公司的执行副主席和总裁、纽约亨利施罗德银行公司总裁和澳大利亚大林公司的总裁。

在到世界银行工作之前，沃尔芬森先生是一名国际投资银行家。他在加入世界银行前的最后一个职位是詹姆斯·D.沃尔芬森公司的总裁和首席执行官，这是他自己于1981年创建的投资公司，主要业务是为美国和外国公司提供咨询。加

---

[2] decorate ['dekəreit] *vt.* 授予（某人）勋章
[3] prior ['praiə] *a.* 优先的，在前的，较早的

relinquished[4] his interests in the firm upon joining the World Bank.

James D. Wolfensohn, the World Bank Group's ninth president since 1946, established his career as an international investment banker with a parallel involvement in development issues and the global environment. On September 27, 1999, Mr. Wolfensohn was unanimously[5] reappointed by the Bank's Board of Executive Directors to a second five-year term as president beginning June 1, 2000. This will make him the third president in World Bank history to serve a second term.

Since becoming president on June 1, 1995, he has traveled to more than 100 countries to gain first-hand experience of the challenges facing the World Bank, and its 183 member countries. During his travels, Mr. Wolfensohn has not only visited development projects supported by the World Bank, but he has also met with the Bank's government clients as well as with representatives from business, labor, media, non-governmental organizations (NGOs), religious and women's groups, students and teachers. In the process he has taken the initiative in forming new strategic partnerships between the Bank and the governments it serves, the private sector, civil society, regional

入世界银行后，他放弃了在公司中的权益。

詹姆斯·戴维·沃尔芬森是世界银行集团自1946年成立以来的第九任行长。他作为国际投资银行家开始了职业生涯，同时也参与了全球开发和全球环境事务。1999年9月27日，世界银行执行董事会一致通过沃尔芬森先生连任世界银行行长，从2000年6月1日开始，任期5年，这使沃尔芬森先生成为世界银行历史上第三位连任的行长。

自1995年6月1日担任行长以来，他访问了100多个国家，目的是获取关于世界银行及其183个成员国所面临的挑战的第一手资料。在访问过程中，沃尔芬森先生不仅到由世界银行资助的发展项目区进行现场考察，而且与世界银行借款国的政府以及企业界、工会组织、新闻界、非政府组织、宗教和妇女团体的代表以及学生和教师会面。其间，他倡导世界银行与其所服务的各国政府、私营部门、民间团体、地区开发银行和联合国建立新的战略伙伴关系。

---

4 relinquish [ri'liŋkwiʃ] vt.交出，让给，放弃
5 unanimously [ju(:)'næniməsli] ad.全体一致地，无异议地

development banks and the UN.

In 1996, together with the International Monetary Fund (IMF), Mr. Wolfensohn initiated the Heavily Indebted Poor Countries Initiative (HIPC) as the first comprehensive debt reduction program to address the needs of the world's poorest, most heavily indebted countries. Two years later, he led a global review of the HIPC Initiative, involving church groups, NGOs and representatives from creditor and HIPC countries, to assess its progress and identify ways to make the Initiative deeper, broader and faster. This review, and proposals by donor countries, culminated[6] in September 1999 with an official endorsement[7] at the World Bank/IMF Annual Meetings to double the amount of relief, make more countries eligible[8] for assistance, and speed up the process.

In January 1999, Mr. Wolfensohn introduced the Comprehensive Development Framework (CDF), drawing on the lessons of development experience and putting into action the key concepts laid out in his Annual Meetings speeches of 1997 and 1998. Together with the Bank's partners, the CDF is now being piloted[9] in 13 countries.

1996年，沃尔芬森先生与国际货币基金组织一起提出了"重债穷国计划"的动议，这是解决世界上最贫困、负债最多的国家的第一个全面的减债计划。两年以后，他又在全球范围领导了对"重债穷国计划"的评议，吸收教会、非政府组织、债权国和重债穷国的代表共同对该动议的进展情况进行评估，寻找进一步深化、扩大和加速其进程的途径。这一评议活动以及各捐助国的建议在1999年9月达到顶点，在世界银行和国际货币基金组织的联合年会上正式批准把救助金额增加一倍，使更多的国家有资格申请援助，并加快了减债的进程。

1999年1月，沃尔芬森先生根据发展的经验教训提出了全面发展框架（CDF），把他在1997年和1998年年会上的讲话中提出的主要观点付诸行动。目前，世界银行正与各个合作伙伴一起在13个国家进行全面发展框架的试点。

---

6 culminate ['kʌlmineit] vt.&vi. 达到极点
7 endorsement [in'dɔːsmənt] n.赞同，支持
8 eligible ['elidʒəbl] a. 有资格当选的，有条件被选中的
9 pilot ['pailət] vt. 引导，指导

The CDF is meant to be a compass — not a blueprint. It is an approach that places the country front and center and focusing on building stronger partnerships to reduce poverty. It has been discussed with a wide variety of audiences including ministers and senior officials of both developed and developing countries, academics, civil society and the private sector, and other stakeholders[10]. Also, a network of CDF focal points within multilateral, bilateral and UN agencies have been meeting regularly on various aspects of implementation.

Throughout his career, Mr. Wolfensohn has also closely involved himself in a wide range of cultural and volunteer activities, especially in the performing arts. In 1970, Mr. Wolfensohn became involved in New York's Carnegie Hall, first as a board member and later, from 1980 to 1991, as Chairman of the Board, during which time he led its successful effort to restore the landmark New York building. He is now Chairman Emeritus[11] of Carnegie Hall. In 1990, Mr. Wolfensohn became Chairman of the Board of Trustees of the John F. Kennedy Center for the Performing Arts in Washington, DC. On January 1, 1996, he was elected Chairman Emeritus.

全面发展框架旨在提供一个指南而不是一份蓝图，旨在把国家放在减贫的核心领导地位，建立更强大的合作伙伴关系。世界银行就全面发展框架与发达国家和发展中国家的部长和高级官员、学者、民间团体、私营部门以及其他各利益相关方开展了广泛讨论。此外，各个多边、双边和联合国机构都有全面发展框架联络官，他们定期开会研究各方面的实施情况。

在他的职业生涯中，沃尔芬森先生也广泛参与一系列的文化和志愿活动，特别是表演艺术领域。1970年，沃尔芬森先生开始参与卡内基音乐厅的工作，他先是卡内基音乐厅的董事，1980年至1991年担任董事会主席，其间，他成功地领导了作为纽约的标志性建筑的卡内基音乐厅的修复工作。他现在是卡内基音乐厅董事会荣誉主席。1990年，沃尔芬森先生成为华盛顿约翰·肯尼迪表演艺术中心理事会主席，并于1996年1月1日当选为理事会名誉主席。

---

[10] stakeholder ['steikhəuldə] *n.* 赌金保管者
[11] emeritus [i(:)'meritəs] *a.* 名誉退休的

财经宝库

1. The UN，联合国。联合国是一个世界性、综合性的政府间国际组织，现有192个会员国。工作语言有阿拉伯语、汉语、英语、法语、俄语、西班牙语。现任秘书长是潘基文。

2. Heavily Indebted Poor Countries Initiative（HIPC），"重债穷国计划"。世界银行和国际货币基金组织于1996年联手推出的一项 "重债穷国计划"（Heavily Indebted Poor Countries Initiative，简称HIPC计划），目的是减少穷国所须偿还的债务。这项计划是通过减轻有关国家的债务，让它们在受到最少干扰的情况下持续发展经济，保持国民生活水平及逐步解决国内的贫困问题。

3. New York's Carnegie Hall, 纽约的卡内基音乐厅。它是有百年历史的音乐殿堂，一度传来要改建的消息，是小提琴家伊萨·斯坦因力挽狂澜把它保存下来。你若去过这座音乐厅，就会

联合国总部大厦

在走廊上看到挂满曾经在此献艺的无数大师的照片。一个新人只要登上卡内基音乐厅，就意味着他的地位已经确立。

DIY工作室

1. Why was Mr. Wolfensohn unanimously reappointed by the World Bank's Board of Executive Directors to a second five-year term as president in 1999?

2. Can you say something about Mr. Wolfensohn's interests in other fields?

归类记忆卡片

股票出借人 stock lender	股权 equity; shareholding
股票期货 stock futures	股票归还 stock return
保荐人 sponsor	保证金价值 margin value
保本产品 capital preservation product	保证基金 Guarantee Fund
非经常项目 extraordinary item	信用评级 credit rating
非金钱利益 soft-dollar benefits	信息交流 exchange of information
子公司 subsidiary	受托人 trustee
金融期货 financial futures	信贷风险 credit risk
金融机构 financial institution	前收市价 previous closing price
金融市场 financial market	后勤办公室 back office

听力广场

James D. Wolfensohn's Philanthropy

Princeton, N.J, May 7, 2007

James D. Wolfensohn will step down as Chairman of the Board of Trustees of the Institute

世界银行前行长詹姆斯·戴维·沃尔芬森的慈善事业

2007年10月，作为高级研究学会的理事会主席，詹姆斯 D. 沃尔

for Advanced Study in October 2007 after twenty-one years of distinguished[12] service to the institution. Under Mr. Wolfensohn's leadership, the Institute has sustained and enhanced its standing as one of the world's leading centers for intellectual inquiry and theoretical research. He will be succeeded for one year by Board Vice-Chairman Martin L. Leibowitz, who will serve as interim[13] Chairman before Charles Simonyi, current President of the Corporation, officially begins as Chairman in October 2008. Mr. Wolfensohn will become Chairman Emeritus effective October 2007.

Peter Goddard, Director of the Institute, stated, "Over many years, Wolfensohn has been an essential force in the development of the Institute, deeply committed to its mission of the disinterested[14] pursuit of knowledge. His vision has guided our growth and evolution as an institution, ensuring the maintenance of the highest standards of excellence and the relevance of the Institute's work. Despite his many other formidable responsibilities, Jim's loyalty and commitment to the Institute have never wavered. He is much loved by the whole Institute community and we owe him an inestimable[15] debt.

芬森在为这个机构作出21年杰出贡献之后将要离任。在沃尔芬森的领导下，这个学院保持并加强了它作为一个世界领先的学术咨询和理论研究的中心位置。在查尔斯·西蒙尼（现在的公司总裁）2008年正式担任主席之前，由现任的副主席马丁·莱伯维茨临时担任一年。沃尔芬森将任名誉主席，2007年10月生效。

学会主任彼得·格达德说："很多年以来，沃尔芬森在学会的发展上成为必不可少的力量，献身于对知识的无私追求。他的远见引导我们学会的成长及发展，以确保维持学会的最高水准以及学会工作的关联。除了他的令人敬佩的责任感，吉姆对于学会的忠诚和承诺从来没有动摇过。他受到学会全体人员的爱戴，我们无法报答他。我们也很高兴马丁·莱伯维茨在这个过渡期同意接任吉姆的工作。马丁也因为他对学会的大力支持和不懈努力而受到人们尊敬。我们都很尊重

---

[12] distinguished [disˈtiŋgwiʃt] a.卓越的，著名的，受人尊敬的
[13] interim [ˈintərim] a.暂时的，临时的
[14] disinterested [diˈsintristid] a.公正的，无私的
[15] inestimable [inˈestiməbl] a.无价的，无法估计的

We are delighted that Marty Leibowitz has agreed to follow Jim as Chairman in this time of transition. Marty is greatly admired for his strong support of the Institute and his unstinting efforts on its behalf. We all respect greatly his wisdom and understanding of the Institute and its work."

他的智慧以及他对学会和其工作的理解。"

Regarding the transition[16], Mr. Wolfensohn noted, "It is always great for an organization to improve its leadership, and with Marty Leibowitz and with Charles Simonyi, the Institute takes a step up and a step forward. I am thrilled to be succeeded by two such extraordinary people."

关于这次交接，沃尔芬森说："对于一个组织来说，改善领导是很重要的，有马丁·莱伯维茨和查尔斯·西蒙尼担任领导，学会将会向更高、更远处发展。看到有这两个杰出的人能继任我的位置，我非常激动。"

Mr. Wolfensohn, former President of The World Bank and current Chairman of Wolfensohn & Company, L.L.C., has been a Trustee of the Institute since 1979 and Chairman of the Board since 1986. Over the past quarter century, Mr. Wolfensohn has helped steward[17] the growth of the Institute's endowment[18], which has more than quadrupled[19] since his appointment as Chairman. He has also taken a particularly active interest in extending the

沃尔芬森先生，世界银行前行长，现任沃尔芬森公司主席，从1979年以来一直是学会的理事，1986年成为理事会主席至今。在过去的25年里，沃尔芬森帮助管理学会的捐助财物，自从他被任命学会主席以来，这个数字翻了两番。他还致力于扩大学会的全球影响和知名度。他和前任学会董事（1991—2003）、现任的数学学院教授菲利普·格利菲斯一起，着手创立千禧

---

[16] transition [træn'ziʃən] *n.* 过渡，转变
[17] steward [stjuəd] *v.* 管理
[18] endowment [in'daumənt] *n.* 资助，捐助；捐助的财物等
[19] quadruple ['kwɔdrupl] *a.* 四倍的

global impact and profile of the Institute. With former Institute Director (1991–2003) and current School of Mathematics Professor Phillip Griffiths, he worked to initiate the Millennium Science Initiative, a program that aims to create and nurture world-class science and scientific talent in the developing world.

Mr. Wolfensohn, together with his wife Elaine, has been an energetic supporter of the Institute's IAS/Park City Mathematics Institute (PCMI), and has also led building projects such as Simonyi Hall (1993) and Bloomberg Hall (2002), which respectively house the Institute's Schools of Mathematics and Natural Sciences. The Institute's lecture and performance hall, Wolfensohn Hall, was dedicated in 1993 in honor of Mr. Wolfensohn, and is a reflection of both his long-standing commitment to the Institute, and his own personal love of music. Mr. and Mrs. Wolfensohn have been actively engaged in the Institute's academic and community activities, and will continue their involvement after Mr. Wolfensohn steps down as Chairman.

The Institute, founded in 1930, is a private, independent academic institution located in Princeton, New Jersey. Its more than 5,000 former Members hold positions of intellectual and scientific leadership in the United States and abroad. Some twenty-one Nobel Laureates, and thirty-four out of forty-eight Fields Medalists, have been Institute Faculty, Members or Visitors.

年科学项目，这是一项旨在在发展中国家发掘并培养世界级的科学天才的项目。

沃尔芬森先生和他的夫人伊莱恩都很支持IAS学会和帕克城数学学会，而且还组织了一些建筑工程，比如西蒙尼厅（1993年）和布鲁姆伯格厅（2002年），这分别为学会的数学学院和自然科学学院提供办公地点。学会的报告和演出厅，沃尔芬森厅，是为了感谢沃尔芬森，于1993年建造，这也反映了他对学会的长期贡献和他个人对音乐的热爱。沃尔芬森夫妇积极参与学院的学术和公益活动，在沃尔芬森先生离任后，他们还会一如既往，积极参与这些活动。

这个学会，位于新泽西州普林斯顿，成立于1930年，是一个私人的、独立的学会。大概有5,000多名前会员在美国和国际上的学术和科学领域起着领导作用，大约21名诺贝尔奖得主及48个菲尔兹奖章获得者的34人都曾经是学会的老师、成员或访问学者。很多沃尔夫数学

Many winners of the Wolf or MacArthur prizes have also been affiliated[20] with the Institute. | 奖或者麦克阿瑟天才基金奖的获奖者也是该学会的成员。

1. Nobel Laureates,诺贝尔奖获得者。诺贝尔奖是以瑞典著名化学家、工业家、硝化甘油炸药发明人阿尔弗雷德·贝恩哈德·诺贝尔(1833—1896)的部分遗产作为基金创立的。诺贝尔奖包括金质奖章、证书和奖金。

2. Fields Medalists，菲尔兹奖章获得者。菲尔兹奖是以已故的加拿大数学家、教育家J.C.菲尔兹(Fields）的姓氏命名的，中文全名为约翰·查尔斯·菲尔兹。菲尔兹奖是最著名的世界性数学奖，由于诺贝尔奖没有数学奖，因此也有人将菲尔兹奖誉为数学中的"诺贝尔奖"。

阿尔弗雷德·贝恩哈德·诺贝尔

3. Wolf prize，沃尔夫奖，1976年1月1日，R.沃尔夫（Ricardo Wolf）及其家族捐献一千万美元成立了沃尔夫基金会，其宗旨主要是促进全世界科学、艺术的发展。R.沃尔夫1887年生于德国，其父是德国汉诺威的一位五金商人，也是该城犹太社会的名流。R.沃尔夫曾在德国研究化学，并获得博士学位。第一次世界大战前移居古巴。他用了将近20年的时间，经过大量试验，历尽艰辛，成功地发明了一种从熔炼废渣中回收铁的方法，从而成为百万富翁。沃尔夫奖主要是奖励对推动人类科学与艺术文明作出杰出贡献的人士，每年评选一次。著名华人数学家陈省身教授就曾于1984年5月获得沃尔夫奖，成为唯一获此殊荣的华人。

---

[20] affiliate [ə'filieit] *vt.* 使隶属于，接纳……为成员

4. MacArthur prize, 麦克阿瑟天才基金奖,该奖项创立于1981年，为纪念银行生命灾难公司的创始人约翰·麦克阿瑟而命名。麦克阿瑟基金会总部设在芝加哥，麦克阿瑟天才基金奖颁给在各个领域内有创意的优秀人才，奖金50万美元，获奖者可自由支配。由于天才奖通过匿名提名评选，既不要求个人申请，也不面谈，事先毫不知情的获奖者面对天上掉下的荣誉和巨额奖金，往往不知所措。

Zhou Xiaochuan

Unit 11

Zhou Xiaochuan
中国人民银行行长：周小川

主题札记

　　周小川现年60岁，不但爱好西方歌剧，善打网球，也是身居如此高位并在西方学术期刊上发表过论文的唯一一位中国官员。就是这位央行行长，其言行牵动着全球经济的神经。

　　周小川试图用基于市场的手段，比如说利率调整，来给过热的中国经济降温，而不是采用限制银行信贷等行政性举措。

　　20世纪90年代初期曾与周小川共事的伊莲娜·拉罗什认为，周小川是一位少见的深思熟虑并颇有天赋的人，他遵循自己思维力量的引导。她说，周小川谙熟经济学，这对中国来说至关重要（伊莲娜·拉罗什当时是摩根士丹利与中国建设银行合资成立的投资机构的首席执行官）。

阅读长廊

Zhou Xiaochuan, one of China's most able technocrats

Dr. Zhou Xiaochuan is a Chinese economist, reformist and technocrat. As governor of the People's Bank of China, he is in charge of the monetary policy of the People's Republic of China.

Zhou Xiaochuan was born in 29 January 1948, in Dongan, Heilongjiang province.

Zhou Xiaochuan graduated from Beijing Chemical Engineering Institute in 1975 and received a Ph.D. degree in economic systems engineering from Qinghua University in 1985.

By 1986, he was advising the State Council on economic restructuring as a member of the Economic Policy Group of the State Council and Deputy Director of the Institute of Chinese Economic Reform Research. He served as Assistant Minister of Foreign Trade from 1986 to 1989 and, between 1986 and 1991, was also a member of the National Committee of Economic

周小川:中国最有能力的技术官员之一

周小川博士是中国经济学家，改革者和技术官员。作为中国人民银行行长，他主管中华人民共和国的货币政策。

周小川1948年1月29日出生于黑龙江省东安县。

周小川1975年毕业于北京化工学院，1985年毕业于清华大学，获得系统工程博士学位。

1986年，周小川任国务院经济政策领导小组成员，并兼任中国经济体制改革研究所副所长，他建议国务院进行经济体制改革。1986年至1989年任对外经济贸易部部长助理，1986年至1991年还任国家经济体制改革委员会委员。

Reform.

In December 2002, he was appointed to his present position as governor of the People's Bank of China. As leading banking authority, Zhou is in charge of clearing up some $865 billion bad loans in the Chinese banking system. He has also been under pressure from the finance ministers and central bankers of the G-7 countries, to revalue[1] the renminbi and change its exchange rate-setting mechanism.

Zhou has published a dozen monographs and over one hundred academic articles in Chinese and international journals. His articles "Rebuilding the relationship between the enterprise and the bank", "Social security: reform and policy recommendations" and book *Marching toward an open economic system* have all won awards in China.

He is generally considered one of the most academically capables of the current Chinese leadership, being praised for his intellect and diplomacy. He has been called "China's most able technocrat" and is the only highly-ranked Chinese politician to have been published in a Western academic journal. Although he is one of the leading policymakers of China, Zhou has kept a relatively low public profile. He doesn't give interviews, and is most famous for the motto:

2002年12 月，周小川被任命为中国人民银行行长。作为领导银行业的管理当局，他负责处理中国银行系统8,650亿美元逾期未还的贷款。那时，他又面临七国集团财政部部长和中央银行行长的压力，他们要求人民币升值，并改变中国原有的汇率形成机制。

周小川在国内和国外刊物上已发表了十多篇专题文章以及一百多篇学术论文。他的文章"重塑企业和银行的关系"、"社会保障：改革和政策建议"以及著作《走向开放型经济体系》都在中国获奖。

他的才智和外交才能都受到普遍赞赏，他被认为是现代中国领导人中最有学术水平的官员之一。他被称做"中国最有能力的技术官员"，也是唯一一个在西方学术刊物上发表文章的中国高层政治家。虽然他是中国决策者之一，但他总是保持比较低调的公众形象。他不经常接受采访，他的一个很有名的座右铭是 "如果市场能够解决问题，就让市场去做。我只是一个裁

---

[1] revalue[ˌriːˈvæljuː:]*vt.&vi.* 调高（货币的）兑换价，使（货币）升值

"If the market can solve the problem, let the market do it. I am just a referee. I am neither a sportsman nor a coach."

The head of China's central bank, Zhou Xiaochuan, has spent the past five years cleaning up China's banks and easing the way for foreign financial firms to take a bigger role in the country.

Unlike the US Federal Reserve, China's governor doesn't make the ultimate decisions on interest rates."Mr. Zhou did a wonderful job given the constraints[2]. On the other hand, it will continue to be a challenge for his successor," says Frank Gong, J.P. Morgan Chase & Co.'s chief economist for China. Sooner or later, he adds, "China has to sort out the question of how much independence the central bank can have."

Mr. Zhou has earned respect as an activist willing to goad[3] a system. With politicians in the US pushing China to make its currency convertible[4], he presided over the most significant change to the system in a decade—allowing the yuan to fluctuate[5] within narrow bands against the dollar and other currencies. The result has

判，我既不是运动员，也不是教练"。

自五年前担任中国央行行长以来，周小川不断推进对银行业的整顿，对希望更多参与中国市场的外资金融机构放宽了限制。

与美国联邦储备委员会不同，中国的央行行长对利率没有最终决定权。摩根大通(J.P. Morgan Chase & Co.)中国首席经济学家龚方雄(Frank Gong)说："鉴于这些制约，周小川的表现可谓非常出色。另一方面，他的继任者还将继续面临挑战。"龚方雄称："中国早晚要面对央行应该有多大独立性的问题。"

周小川因积极推动银行系统的发展而赢得了尊敬。在美国政治家向中国施压、要求人民币实现可自由兑换时，他主持了10年来中国银行系统最重要的一次变化——允许人民币兑美元和其他货币在一个狭窄的区间内波动。此后，人民币逐步升值，不过，美国一些国会议员

---

[2] constraint[kən'streint] *n.* 强制，限制，约束
[3] goad[gəud] *vt.* 刺激，激励
[4] convertible[kən'vətəbl] *a.* (货币)可自由兑换的
[5] fluctuate['flʌktjueit] *vi.* 波动，涨落，起伏

been a stronger yuan, although some in the US Congress say China needs to allow its currency to rise much further.

Mr. Zhou, a 60-year-old economist who has published his work in a Western academic journal, is viewed as one of few Chinese leaders with a firm grasp of how financial markets work. He has also become a recognized international spokesman for China's economic policies, giving speeches in English.

Among the changes he advocated[6] were letting foreign banks set up branches in China and helping three of China's major banks list overseas.

The changes aren't popular with some in the leadership who believe Chinese firms may be threatened by the greater access given to foreigners. Also, some officials think China has focused too much on financial liberalization and not enough on rural development.

"There was a lot of pressure on the central-bank governor to fix the nonperforming loans of the banks. Zhou managed to clean them up and now they are reporting record profits," says Zhao Xijun, deputy director of the School of Finance at Renmin University of China and an

宣称中国应允许人民币更进一步升值。

周小川，一位60岁的经济学家，曾在西方学术刊物上发表经济文章，他被视为中国少数能真正领会金融市场运行机制的高官之一。他也是公认的中国经济政策的国际发言人，他可以用英语发表讲话。

他推动的变革还有允许外资银行在中国设立分行，批准中国三家国有银行到海外上市。

有些官员并不愿看到这种变化，他们认为对外资进入中国放宽限制可能威胁到中国企业。还有一些官员认为，中国过于关注对金融业的自由化，而对农村地区的发展重视得不够。

中国人民大学财政金融学院副院长、政府金融政策顾问赵锡军说："央行行长在解决银行不良贷款问题上面临很大压力。周小川成功解决了这个问题，现在这些银行都实现了创纪录的利润。"

---

[6] advocate['ædvəkeit] v. 提倡，主张

adviser to the government on financial policies.

A shorter-term issue: how to respond if the slowing US economy has a more serious downturn. China has been raising interest rates to curb[7] inflation, but it might need to loosen monetary policy to keep its own growth on track.

近期的问题是，如果美国经济出现更严重的下滑，中国应如何应对。中国已多次提高利率以遏制通货膨胀，但为了保持经济继续增长，它可能需要采取宽松的货币政策。

财经宝库

1. technocrat，技术官员，"中国最有能力的技术官员"，英国《金融时报》曾这样来描述周小川。"技术官员"，这个国人并不习惯的称谓，是海外对中国各级政府中大量拥有专业背景的中高层官员阶层的俗称。

2. the US Federal Reserve, 美国联邦储备委员会，是联邦储备系统的核心机构。

3. J.P. Morgan Chase & Co. 摩根大通公司，其总部位于纽约，它为3,000多万名消费者以及企业、机构和政府客户提供服务。该公司拥有7,930亿美元资产，业务遍及50多个国家，是投资银行业务、金融服务、金融事务处理、投资管理、私人银行业务和私募股权投资方面的领导者。摩根大通（J.P. Morgan Chase& Co.）为全球历史最长、规模最大的金融服务集团之一，由大通银行、J.P.摩根公司及富林明集团在2000年合并形成。

摩根大通公司大楼

---

[7] curb[kə:b] *vt.* 限制，克制，抑制

DIY工作室

1. What's your opinion of Mr. Zhou Xiaochuan's economic policy?

2. Do you think it is necessary for China to raise interest rates in order to curb inflation?

归类记忆卡片

尾盘 at-the-close order

技术分析 technical analysis

投资级别 investment grade

投资顾问 investment adviser

投标程序 tender procedure

每日价格上限 daily trading limit

私有化/私营化 privatization

系统性风险 systematic risk

亚洲美元市场 Asian dollar market

到期日 expiration date

制裁权 power of sanction

协议安排 scheme of arrangement

受益人 beneficiary

垃圾债券 junk bond

定期债券 term bond

经常账户 current account

放宽管制 deregulation

资产注入 asset injection

股份权益 share entitlements

股东权益 equity interest

听力广场

Progress achieved in China's market-based interest rate reform and problems remained

By Zhou Xiaochuan

The Chinese Communist Party and Government attach great importance to the market-based interest rate reform. In 1993, the 3rd Plenum of the 14th CPC National Congress pointed out that "the central bank shall promptly adjust benchmark interest rate according to changes in market supply and demand, and allow the commercial banks to flexibly set their own rate on loans and deposits within a specified range". The 5th Plenum of the 15th CPC National Congress in 2000 and the 4th Plenum of the 9th National People's Congress in 2001 called for "steady progress in market-based interest rate reform". In 2002, the 16th CPC National Congress adopted in its report the decision to "steadily advance market-based interest rate reform and optimize the allocation of financial resources". The *Decision on Issues Concerning Improving the Socialist Market Economic*

中国利率市场化改革的成果及存在的问题

　　党和政府高度重视利率市场化改革。早在1993年，十四届三中全会已经提出"中央银行按照资金供求状况及时调整基准利率，并允许商业银行存贷款利率在规定幅度内自由浮动"，2000年的十五届五中全会、2001年九届全国人大四次会议提出要"稳步推进利率市场化改革"，2002年十六大报告中进一步提出"稳步推进利率市场化改革，优化金融资源配置"。2003年10月召开了党的十六届三中全会，通过了《中共中央关于完善社会主义市场经济体制若干问题的决定》，进一步明确要"稳步推进利率市场化，建立健全由市场供求决定的利率形成机制，中央银行通过运用货币政策工具引导市场利率"。

System adopted by the 3rd Plenum of the 16th CPC National Congress further pointed out that "market-based interest rate reform should be steadily advanced to establish and improve the mechanism for determining interest rate based on market supply and demand. The central bank shall use monetary instruments to influence market interest rate".

While moving in the general direction of market-based interest rate reform, we need to clarify some concepts. Some people think that the objective of market-based interest rate reform is to let all interest rates determined by the market. This perception is incorrect. The interest rates that will be determined by the market include commercial rates but not the interest rates used by the central bank to conduct financial management.

In recent years, China's market-based interest rate reform has advanced steadily, with significant progress achieved in the deregulation of money market interest rate. First, market has been playing an increasingly important role in determining the types of interest rate in the money market, which now include inter-bank lending rate, bond repurchase rate, bill market discount rate, interest rate in the primary and secondary market of government bond and policy financial bond. Second, management of interest rate on loans and deposits has been streamlined. The previous practice of regulating

基于市场的利率改革这一总的方向明确以后，我们需要澄清一些概念上的认识。有人以为，利率市场化改革的目标就是让所有利率都由市场决定。这个理解不正确。应当说，利率市场化指的是商业性利率由市场决定，而中央银行进行宏观调控所运用的利率不在此列。

近年来，我国利率市场化改革稳步推进，特别是货币市场利率放开的进度比较快，利率市场化改革取得了阶段性成果。一是逐步实现货币市场利率品种的市场化，包括银行同业拆借利率、债券回购利率、票据市场转贴现利率、国债与政策性金融债券的发行利率和二级市场利率等。二是不断简化存贷款利率管理。过去管理的利率品种很多，近年来，通过放开或取消管制，提高了商业银行管理利率的自主性。三是先后三次扩大对中小企业贷款的利率浮动幅度，增强了银

most types of interest rate has been changed and commercial banks have been given greater flexibility in managing the interest rate. Third, the floating band of interest rate on loans to small and medium sized enterprises has been widened for three times, leading to improved risk management capability of the banks and enabling these enterprises to have easier access to bank credit. Fourth, management of interest rate on foreign currency has been relaxed. At present, there are only a few types of foreign currency interest rate that are still subject to the central bank management. Fifth, domestic commercial banks have introduced large amount time deposit business for domestic insurance companies, with the interest rate jointly determined by both sides.

Despite the above progress, China's market-based interest rate reform has lagged behind the overall economic reform and opening up. One of the major reasons is lack of proper understanding of the reform. For example, when talking about the level of interest rate, some people tend to think it is solely determined by the cost of fund, without giving due consideration to market supply and demand. This is similar to the improper understanding of the factors determining the price of goods in the early stage of reform. In addition, some people have not established the concept of risk premium when considering the level of interest rate. The need

行贷款的风险管理能力，缓解了中小企业贷款难问题。四是放开了对外币利率的管理。目前，人民银行管理的外币利率品种已经很少了。五是中资商业银行对中资保险公司试行大额定期存款业务，利率由双方协商确定。

然而，相对于中国经济改革和对外开放的整体步伐而言，利率市场化改革进展较慢。认识没有跟上是一个重要原因，比如，一提到利率水平高低，有人会习惯性地从资金成本上找答案，而不是从市场供求的角度去考虑。这与我们改革早期进行商品价格改革时对价格形成机制的理解犯有同样的毛病。再有，一些人在利率水平的价格决定机制中缺乏对风险补偿的考虑，还没有建立风险升水的概念。此外，中小企业改革任务艰巨，需要利率政策给予适当的扶持也是影响利率水平的一个因素。

for favourable interest rate policy to support the reform of small and medium-sized enterprises is also a factor affecting the level of interest rate.

1. CPC National Congress，中国共产党全国代表大会。
2. the 4th Plenum of the 9th National People's Congress，九届全国人大四次会议。

Michael Steinhardt

Unit 12

Michael Steinhardt

世界级短线杀手：迈克尔·斯坦哈特

主题札记

　　迈克尔·斯坦哈特，一个白手起家的亿万富翁、世界级短线杀手。1967年，他在纽约建立了以自己名字命名的投资管理公司，28年后，斯坦哈特关闭了26亿美元的合伙投资基金，全身引退转而投身于公益慈善事业。如果谁在1967年投入斯坦哈特公司1万美元，那么20年后就可以拥有100万美元。他被尊为"全球避险基金教父"，是华尔街历史上最成功的基金经理人之一。他善于买空、卖空，一向以果断激进的投资风格著称，是当之无愧的世界级短线大师。迈克尔·斯坦哈特非常成功地驾驭了牛市与熊市，为自己和他的投资人赚了大钱。1995年关闭基金后，他的成功在慈善事业中得到了继续。迈克尔·斯坦哈特给人最深刻的印象是他干劲十足、不计付出。

阅读长廊

Michael Steinhardt and His "Birthright Israel"

Michael H. Steinhardt was born on December 7, 1940, in Brooklyn, New York, is an American businessman and philanthropist active in Jewish causes. He was one of the first prominent hedge fund managers. He founded Steinhardt, Fine, Berkowitz & Co., a hedge fund, in 1967.

Steinhardt averaged an annualized return for his clients of 24.5%, after a 1% management fee and a "performance fee" of 15% (early in his career, later 20%) of all annual gains, nearly triple the annualized performance of the S & P 500 index over the same time frame.

Steinhardt has been an active philanthropist, donating over $125 million to Jewish causes. I had anticipated speaking with Michael Steinhardt primarily about "birthright Israel", the 10-days-in-Israel program for 18-26-year-olds. He co-

迈克尔·斯坦哈特和他的"以色列生存权"项目

迈克尔·斯坦哈特1940年12月7日生于纽约布鲁克林，是美国著名商人、慈善家，热心犹太人事业。他是著名的对冲基金经理之一。1967年他创立了斯坦哈特·法恩·博克维兹对冲基金公司。

在扣除管理费1%和劳务费15%（前期是15%，后期是20%）之后，斯坦哈特平均每年给他的客户24.5%的回报率，跟同时期的标准普尔指数相比，几乎是它的三倍。

斯坦哈特是一个积极的慈善家，捐款1.25亿美元给犹太人事业。我一直期望能跟迈克尔·斯坦哈特谈一谈"以色列生存权"项目，那是一个为18至26岁的犹太年

founded and has so heavily underwritten[1], and which, astoundingly[2], is about to welcome its 100,000th participant.

And birthright was indeed what we started off discussing. It has been, Steinhardt happily and rightly reported, a staggering[3] success, a transformative experience for those who come here, to the point where one of its biggest problems right now is that the program simply cannot keep pace with the worldwide demand to join it.

Steinhardt estimates that perhaps 50,000 more youngsters are waiting to come on birthright trips than can be accommodated[4] in the near future. One solution, of course, might be to adjust the innovation at its financial heart—that participants need pay absolutely nothing, with all costs underwritten by a partnership of the Israeli government, Jewish federations and private philanthropy. But Steinhardt wouldn't dream of it. Instead the principals have set up a birthright foundation, to raise additional revenues, toward a goal of doubling, at least, the 21,000 places available to participants this year.

If birthright can get its annual numbers

轻人提供为期10天的在以色列游历的项目，是斯坦哈特和其他人共同创办的，但他自己承担很大费用。令人震惊的是，这个项目将接受第10万个参与者。

生存权的确是我们开始讨论的话题。斯坦哈特高兴又肯定地说，生存权是一个难以置信的成功，对于那些来到这里的人们来说，意义非同寻常。简单地说，现在最大的问题是这个项目不能满足世界范围内想加入这个项目的所有人的要求。

斯坦哈特估计，在不久的将来，除了他们可以提供住处的人数以外，可能还有约5万多名年轻人等着通过这个项目到这里来。当然，一种解决办法就是要调整改革这个计划的财政要点，也就是，参与者不用付任何费用，所有的费用由以色列政府、犹太教联合会和私人慈善赞助联合承担。但是斯坦哈特不会只停留在梦想上。相反，负责人已经设立了一个生存权基金会，想加大收入，目标是争取使生存权参与者扩大到至少现在的21,000个地方的两倍。

他估计，如果生存权项目每年

---

[1] underwrite ['ʌndərait] vt. 签名同意支付；同意负担……费用
[2] astoundingly[əs'taundiŋli] ad. 使人震惊地
[3] staggering['stægriŋ] a.难以置信的；令人震惊的
[4] accommodate[ə'kɔmədeit] v. 向……提供住处

above 40,000, he reckons[5], this would enable about half of the Jewish youngsters worldwide in its age group to take advantage of the program—an extraordinary ambition.

Birthright emerged from the recognition that Jewish identity is relentlessly[6] weakening among Diaspora[7] youngsters, that an Israel experience is the most potent[8] means of bolstering[9] the Jewish soul, and that if wealthy, capable and innovative individuals—principally Steinhardt and co-founder Charles Bronfman—didn't initiate what amounts to an emergency Diaspora rescue program, nobody else was going to.

Steinhardt—who closed the Wall Street hedge-fund that had made him a reported $300 million fortune a decade ago to devote his time and money primarily to Jewish causes, and has funded Jewish life-enriching projects from Manhattan's Makor singles venture to the Israel Museum— readily acknowledges that 10 days in Israel is not, in itself, the panacea[10] for Diaspora indifference and assimilation[11]. The organizers are constantly striving[12] to improve follow-up programming once participants get back home.

的名额达到4万名以上，那么我们就能让全世界符合年龄的一半以上的犹太年轻人从这个项目受益，这的确是一个宏伟目标。

生存权项目的出现是因为人们意识到在犹太人散居地的年轻人中，犹太人的特性在日渐衰落。他们还意识到，支持犹太精神的最有说服力的事情就是去以色列游历。如果不是那些富有的、能干的、有改革精神的人（主要是斯坦哈特和共同创办人查尔斯·布隆夫曼）着手做这个可以称得上是紧急散居犹太人拯救计划，就不会有别人去做。

斯坦哈特，关闭了他的华尔街对冲基金公司，据说这个公司在10年前为他挣了3亿美元，转而把所有的时间和精力都投向犹太人事业，还资助了犹太生活丰富工程，包括从曼哈顿的迈克个人风险投资到以色列博物馆等。斯坦哈特承认，10天在以色列的游历本身不是治疗散居在外的犹太人不关心本族文化和被异族同化的万能药。不过，一旦参与者回国以后，组织者会不断努力发展一些后续性项目。

---

[5] reckon['rekən] v.猜想，估计

[6] relentlessly[ri'lentlisli] ad.无情地，残酷地

[7] Diaspora[dai'æspərə] n.犹太人在外的聚居区；在外散居的犹太人

[8] potent['pəutənt] a.强有力的，有说服力的

[9] bolster['bəulstə] vt.给予必要的支持，鼓励

[10] panacea[,pænə'siə] n.治百病的药，万能药

[11] assimilation[ə,simi'leiʃən] n.同化（作用）

[12] strive[straiv] vi.努力奋斗，追求

And Steinhardt himself, now in his mid-60s, is deeply engaged in a variety of other "resonant[13] and exciting" educational programs—for preschool, day school and beyond— designed to inculcate[14] Jewish values into youngsters, and their parents, who might otherwise be lost.

By the end of the year, he promises chiefly, he and his philanthropist partners will finally establish a much-anticipated $100 million "Fund for our Jewish Future"—an initiative designed no less than to "transform American Jewish education" and "hopefully begin to create the necessary tools to maintain the Jewish people in the Diaspora in perpetuity[15]. Now, if that sounds optimistic," he smiles, "it probably is."

Choosing his words painstakingly[16], in the softest of tones and with the lengthiest of pauses between some of them, Steinhardt ascribes[17] the "crisis"in North American Jewry, in part, to the very tolerance and shared priorities of the wider, non-Jewish environment. It is the crisis of a community "living as a minority among people whose values have begun to merge[18] with their own," he says, "and who have welcomed them in so many ways as to make difficult their ability

现在已经65岁的斯坦哈特自己也积极参与各种能引起反响的激动人心的教育项目，这些项目是为学前教育、全日制教育等设计旨在把犹太人的价值观反复灌输给年轻人以及他们的父母，否则，这些价值观将会消失。

他承诺，到今年底，他和他的慈善家合作伙伴们最终要建立一个有更多人参与的总值1亿美元的"为了我们犹太人的未来基金"——这个倡议不亚于"改变美国的犹太人教育"，并"希望开始创造必要的条件来永久保持离散地的犹太人之间的联系，如果那听起来比较乐观的话，"他笑着说，"很有可能会是这样。"

他以最温和的语调，有时候会停顿好长时间，小心翼翼地选择他的用词，斯坦哈特把这种北美的犹太人区的"危机"部分归因于犹太人的容忍和能共享的更广范围的非犹太人环境内的优先权。这是社区的危机，"作为一个少数民族生活在一个群体中，他们的价值观会和这些少数人的价值观融合，"他说，"周围的人以各种方式欢迎他们的到来，以至于他们想与周围的

---

13 resonant['rezənənt] a. 反响的，由共鸣而加强的
14 inculcate['inkʌlkeit] vt. 极力主张，反复灌输
15 perpetuity[,pə(:)pi'tju(:)iti] n. 永久，永恒
16 painstakingly['peinz,teikiŋli] ad. 极小心地，辛勤地，辛苦地
17 ascribe[əs'kraib] vt. 把……归于
18 merge[mə:dʒ] vt.&vi. （使）混合，（使）合并

to justify separation. But it also reflects the inability of the Jewish people to communicate their own history and their own values in a resonant enough way from generation to generation, so that even in this extraordinarily warm, seductive[19], inviting environment, they understand why it is really important to be Jewish and why we should take great pride in being Jewish."

One potential solution for Diaspora decline, I posit[20], is surely an observant approach to Judaism[21]—if not via the non-Orthodox streams, then via the Orthodox and ultra-Orthodox, where intermarriage[22] rates are far lower.

Steinhardt's refusal to view Orthodoxy[23] as a remedy for the disappearing Diaspora begs another question. "What then," I ask him across the coffee table of his Tel Aviv hotel room, "are the Jewish values and traits that you are seeking to preserve and maintain in this non-observant Jewish people that you want to educate?"

"I have very strong answers to that," he says. "I particularly, being an atheist[24], have thought a lot about what it is about being Jewish that's worthy of maintaining. Because I think

人分开都很难。但是这也反映了一代又一代的犹太人缺乏足够的能力以一种能引起共鸣的方式来与他们的历史和他们的价值观交流，所以，即使是在这种特别温暖、富有魅力的、吸引人的环境中，他们也应该懂得为什么做一个犹太人是那么重要，为什么我们应该为自己是犹太人而自豪。"

至于离散犹太人的价值观下降的问题，我想，一个可能的解决办法，肯定是要接触犹太教——如果不是通过非正统的方法，就是通过正统的或者极端正统的方法，那样的话，异族通婚率就会低得多。

斯坦哈特拒绝把正统看成是逐渐消失的犹太文化的补救办法这一点，又引起了我的另一个问题，"那么，"我在他的特拉维夫饭店房间隔着桌子问他，"在这些你想教育的不太遵守犹太习俗的人身上，什么是你想要试图维持和保护的犹太人的价值观和特征？"

"我有很明确的答案"，他说，"我，作为一个无神论者，对于值得犹太人保持的东西思考得很多。因为我认为在21世纪我们不断

---

[19] seductive[si'dʌktiv] a.诱人的，富有魅力的
[20] posit['pɔzit] vt. 假定，设想，假设
[21] Judaism['dʒu:deiizəm] n. 犹太教
[22] intermarriage[,intə(:)'mæridʒ] n. 结婚，婚姻状况
[23] orthodoxy['ɔ:θədɔksi] n.正统观念；普遍接受的观点
[24] atheist['eiθiist] n.无神论者

as we extend ourselves in the 21st century, more and more Jews are having a great deal of difficulty in dealing with the idea of a relevant supernatural[25]. I think we have to begin to deeply analyze what it means to be Jewish."

"Historically," he goes on, "it was always comfortable to say 'those who are Jewish believe in the Torah and what's written there,' and it's so God-centric that it answered most of the questions. Today, for most of us, it doesn't answer most of the questions anymore, whether we call ourselves theists or atheists or whatever. It seems to me one has to begin to seriously start asking questions that one didn't have to ask before."

地发展，越来越多的犹太人在处理一些相关的超自然现象方面有很多困难。我认为我们不得不开始分析作为犹太人到底意味着什么。"

"从历史角度讲，"他继续说，"人们很自然地说，'那些犹太人相信犹太经的全部经文和里面写的东西，'那是以上帝为中心的，它能回答绝大部分问题。今天，对于我们大部分人来说，不管我们自己认为是有神论者，或无神论者，或其他什么，它不再能回答大部分的问题。我认为人们必须认真开始问一些以前不必问的问题。"

财经宝库

1. Birthright Israel，"以色列生存权"项目，这是斯坦哈特先生与查尔斯·布隆夫曼共同创立的，此项目旨在给每一个海外犹太青年提供免费游历以色列的机会。

2. Torah，[宗]犹太经的全部经文。

3. Charles Bronfman，查尔斯·布隆夫曼，慈善家，与斯坦哈特一起建立了"以色列生存权"项目。

4. Tel Aviv hotel，特拉维夫，是以色列第二大城市，那里不仅建有很多的酒店，而且有越来越多的游客喜欢去特拉维夫观光和度假。那里拥有良好的住宿条件，沿

---

[25] supernatural[ˌsjuːpəˈnætʃərəl] n.超自然的事物，超自然现象

Hayarkon大街酒店林立，其中不乏五星级豪华酒店。在海滩沿线也有很多五星级高级酒店，特拉维夫酒店就是其中一家。

1. What is "birthright Israel" program co-founded by Michael Steinhardt and Charles Bronfman?

2. What are the Jewish values and traits that Steinhardt is seeking to preserve and maintain in this non-observant Jewish people that he wants to educate?

主权风险 sovereign risk	外围市场 fringe market
世界银行 World Bank	可赎回股份 redeemable share
代客交易 agency trade	外汇敞口 foreign exchange exposure
以股换股 share exchange	外汇基金票据 exchange fund bill
以最佳价格/条件执行交易的原则 principle of best execution	失责人士 defaulter
	失职行为 misconduct
另类投资 alternative investment	市值 market value; capitalization
可用年限 useful life	市场占有率 market share
可转让票据 negotiable instrument	市场风险 market risk
可行性研究 feasibility study	市场参与者 market participant
包销商 underwriter	

Michael Steinhardt's Investment Style

As a teenager, Michael Steinhardt was reading stock charts and hanging around brokerage offices. He finished high school at age 16 and flew through the Wharton School of Finance in three years, graduating in 1960.

He began his career on Wall Street in research and analyst positions with mutual fund company Calvin Bullock and the brokerage firm of Loab Rhoades & Co.. In 1967, Steinhardt, along with two other rising stars in the investment field, Howard Berkowitz and Jerrold Fine, formed a hedge fund company based in New York, which they named Steinhardt, Fine, Berkowitz & Co. Under Steinhardt's direction, the firm was consistently successful in identifying macro market moves and then fitting its securities trading strategies into these situations. In 1979, Berkowitz and Fine left the partnership, which was then renamed as Steinhardt Partners.

Steinhardt's spectacular career ended in 1995 when he decided to close the business

迈克尔·斯坦哈特的投资方式

十几岁的时候，迈克尔·斯坦哈特就开始分析股票交易技术图，在布鲁克林股票交易所闲逛。16岁那年，他完成了高中的学习，考入了（宾夕法尼亚大学）沃顿金融学院，三年以后，1960年就（提前）毕业了。

他在卡尔文·布洛克互助基金公司和罗布·罗兹证券公司里找到了一份证券研究和分析的工作，从而开始了他在华尔街传奇的投资生涯。1967年，斯坦哈特同投资领域另外两名"新星"——霍华德·博克维兹和杰罗德·法恩一起，在纽约创办了对冲基金公司，他们将它起名为斯坦哈特·法恩·博克维兹公司。在斯坦哈特的指导下，公司在辨别宏观市场走向方面一向很成功，然后根据形势调整他们的证券交易策略。1979年，博克维兹和法恩离开了这个合伙公司，后来公司就改名叫斯坦哈特合伙人公司。

斯坦哈特辉煌的投资生涯在1995年结束，在他前一年基金收入

with his fortune and reputation intact[26] after his fund gained 21% in its last year. This was a year removed from the tough loss that he suffered in 1994, when interest rates moved against him, which produced a 30% loss for his fund.

He then turned to philanthropic activities and served as a board member for institutions such as New York University, University of Pennsylvania and Brandeis University. He has also served on the board of Wisdom Tree Investments, a New York-based asset management firm that sponsors exchange-traded funds.

Steinhardt had a long-term investor's perspective but, for the most part, invested as a short-term strategic trader. He bet on directional moves using an eclectic[27] mix of securities and was backed up by a team of traders and analysts. As mentioned above, he emphasized macro asset allocation type moves from which he harvested his gains. Charles Kirk, publisher of The Kirk Report, gleaned[28] these "rules of investing" from a Steinhardt speech back in June, 2004, which show that even a high-flying hedge fund investor needs to be grounded:

1. Make all your mistakes early in life. The more tough lessons early on, the fewer errors you make later.

21%的情况下，他决定关闭他的公司，使他的财产和名誉完好无损。他刚从1994年的失败中挺过来。1994年，由于利率变化跟他作对，他遭受了巨大损失，他的基金损失达30%。

然后他转向慈善活动，担任如纽约大学、宾夕法尼亚大学以及布兰戴大学的董事会成员。他还是智慧树投资公司董事会成员，这是设在纽约的倡导交换基金的管理公司。

斯坦哈特有长期投资家的眼光，但他绝大部分时候是做短线的策略型交易者。他利用证券的混合信息赌股市的方向，并得到了许多交易商和分析师的支持。就像上面提到的，他重视宏观财产分配型基金走向，从中收获颇丰。查尔斯·科克，是《科克报告》的出版商，从斯坦哈特在2004年6月发表的一篇演说中，一点点收集了一些"投资法则"，表明即使是野心勃勃的对冲基金投资者也需要依据这些准则：

1. 犯错要尽早。越早遇到一些深刻的教训，之后你犯的错误就越少。

---

[26] intact[in'tækt] *a.* 完整无缺的，未受损伤的
[27] eclectic[ek'lektik] *a.*（方法、思想等）折中的，从不同来源选辑的
[28] glean[gli:n] *vt.* 一点点地收集（资料、事实）

2. Always make your living doing something you enjoy.

3. Be intellectually competitive. The key to research is to assimilate as much data as possible in order to be to the first to sense a major change.

4. Make good decisions even with incomplete information. You will never have all the information you need. What matters is what you do with the information you have.

5. Always trust your intuition,[29] which resembles a hidden supercomputer in the mind. It can help you do the right thing at the right time if you give it a chance.

6. Don't make small investments. If you're going to put money at risk, make sure the reward is high enough to justify the time and effort you put into the investment decision.

2. 永远做你喜欢的事来营生。

3. 保持智力上的竞争力。研究的重点是要随时研究可能带来财富的一切数据，要比别人更早感知大势的变化。

4. 即使信息不充分也要尽量作恰当的决定。你永远不可能得到你所要的全部信息，关键是怎么把握现有的信息。

5. 永远相信你的直觉。直觉就像你脑子里藏着的超级电脑，如果你给机会，它能帮助你在合适的时间做合适的事情。

6. 不做小投资。如果你冒险投资，请你确信回报足以补偿你为投资决策付出的时间和精力。

非常点拨

1. Calvin Bullock，纽约一家基金公司。

2. Howard Berkowitz and Jerrold Fine，霍华德·博克维兹和杰罗德·法恩，投资领域的佼佼者，他们两人曾和斯坦哈特先生一起在纽约创办了一家对冲基金公司。

3. Wisdom Tree Investments, 智慧树投资公司。

---

[29] intuition[ˌintjuˈiʃən] *n.* 直觉，凭直觉感知的知识

Peter Lynch

Unit 13

Peter Lynch
全球最佳选股者：彼得·林奇

主题札记

　　彼得·林奇是当今美国乃至全球最高薪的投资组合经理人，是麦哲伦100万共同基金的创始人，是杰出的职业股票投资人，华尔街股票市场的聚财巨头。彼得·林奇在其数十年的职业股票投资生涯中，特别是他于1977年接管并扩展麦哲伦基金以来，股票生意做得极为出色，不仅使麦哲伦成为有史以来最庞大的共同基金，其资产由2,000万美元增长到84亿美元，而且使公司的投资配额表上原来仅有的40种股票增长到1,400种。彼得·林奇也因此收获甚丰。惊人的成就使彼得·林奇蜚声金融界。美国最有名的《时代》周刊称他为第一理财专家，《幸福》杂志则称他是股票领域一位超级投资巨星。彼得·林奇从投资经营中也认识到了自己的不凡，并以股票天使自居。

阅读长廊

Peter Lynch is a successful Wall Street investor, and arguably one of the best stock-pickers in the world. He was president of the international investment management firm Fidelity.

Peter was born in 1944 in the USA. He served for two years in the United States Army and studied finance at the Wharton School in the University of Pennsylvania before becoming an analyst in 1969 for the international investment management firm Fidelity. In 1974 Peter was promoted to director of research and took on the Fidelity Magellan fund in 1977. When Peter took on the fund it had $22 million in assets.

Peter took on a grueling[1] work load in which he worked six or seven days a week. During this time he talked to company managers, brokers and analysts every day. With the help of just two research assistants, he ran a portfolio of up

彼得·林奇是一个成功的华尔街投资者，可以说是世界上最佳选股者之一。他是富达国际投资管理公司的总裁。

1944年，彼得·林奇出生于美国。他在美国军队服役两年，后来又在宾夕法尼亚大学沃顿商学院学习金融。1969年进入富达国际投资管理公司成为一名分析师。1974年，彼得被提升为研究部主任，1977年接管富达麦哲伦基金。当彼得接管这个基金的时候，麦哲伦基金的总资产是2,200万美元。

彼得·林奇常常忘我工作，一周工作六天，甚至七天。这段日子他每天都跟公司经理、经纪人和分析师谈话。在只有两个研究助理的帮助下，他同时可以管理1,400种

---

[1] grueling['gruəliŋ] *a.*折磨的，使筋疲力尽的

to 1,400 stocks at any one time. Some of these stocks he bought at an early stage of growth or recovery and held for years, but most of the stocks he bought he became displeased with and sold within months of their purchase, admitting that over half his choices were mistakes.

The Fidelity Magellan fund averaged an amazing 29.2% return a year, and only under-performed the S&P 500 index twice. Peters most impressive investing successes include undervalued companies such as Taco Bell and Pier 1 Imports before periods of strong market growth.

For the 13 years that Peter Lynch managed the Fidelity Magellan Funds, it was the top-ranked general equity mutual fund in America. 1,000 dollars invested in the Magellan fund in 1977 was worth $28,000 when he retired from managing the Magellan fund. In 1990 he decided to take early retirement in order to spend more time with his family, and by that time its value had swollen to $14 billion. He is the only manager that has ever run such a large fund, so successfully, for so long. Peter continues as a member on the board of trustees of the Fidelity Group of funds and also writes a column for *Worth* magazine.

After Peter retired he wrote two books on stock selection, *One Up on Wall Street* in 1989 and *Beating the Street* in 1994. Both of

股票。有些在股市增长初期或恢复期购买的股票，他会持有好几年，但是他对他购买的绝大部分股票都不满意，购买之后几个月他就会把它们卖掉，他承认自己大概有一半以上的选择是错误的。

富达麦哲伦基金一年的平均回报率为惊人的29.2%，只有两次比标准普尔500指数稍差一些。在强劲的市场增长前夕，彼得给人留下印象最深的成功投资是投资了几家市值被低估的公司，如Taco Bell和Pier 1 Imports公司。

在彼得·林奇管理麦哲伦基金的13年中，它是美国第一流的普通共同基金。1977年在麦哲伦基金投资的1,000美元到1990年彼得从该公司退休时，价值能达到28,000美元。1990年，为了能有更多的时间与家人在一起，他决定提前退休，这时，公司总资产已攀升至140亿美元。他是唯一能这么长时间如此成功地管理这么大一个公司的人。虽然离开公司，但他还依然是富达集团理事会成员，还为《价值》杂志写专栏文章。

彼得退休后写了两本关于股票选择的书：1989年的《彼得·林奇的成功投资》和1994年的《战胜华

which are considered essential reading for any serious investor. Peter has found many of his big investments when not in his office — instead found them when out with his family, driving around or shopping at the mall. Peter believes the individual investor is able to do this too.

Peter is adamant[2] that small investors can research stocks better than most professionals, and make smarter decisions about what to buy because they are often in better positions to spot potentially profitable investments early. They are also free to act independently, rather than be constrained[3] by committees, trustees.

The Wall Street guru[4] says that the secret to his success is his ability to "think like an amateur". He offers a common-sense approach to stock picking: Know the "story", or everything about a company, before buying a stock; then follow the "story" after buying the stock. He says, "Don't sell the stock if the 'story' is still good, whether the market is up or down."

To begin to select a "story", find publicly traded companies that provide good products and services. You can begin to gather information for your "story" every time you walk into a mall, go to a restaurant, or play with your

尔街》。这两本书都被认为是任何一个认真投资者的基础读物。彼得有很多大的投资不是在他的办公室里发现的——相反，是他在和家人外出时，开车出去闲逛或在商场购物时发现的。彼得相信个体投资者都能做到这一点。

彼得相信，小投资者往往比大部分专业人士更能研究股票。关于该买什么样的股票，他们常常能作出更明智的决定，因为他们所处的位置更能早日看到有潜力的有利可图的投资。他们独立行动起来也更自由，而不会被委员会或委托人所束缚。

华尔街的领袖称，彼得的成功秘诀在于他能够"像一个外行一样思考"。他提供了一个选股的通俗办法：在买股票前，要了解"故事"，或者说是关于公司的一切；然后在购买之后要一直跟踪这个"故事"。他说："不管市场是上升还是下降，如果'故事'还是好的，就不要卖掉。"

开始选择"故事"时，要选择能提供好的产品和好的服务的公共交易公司。每次你走进一个商场，去一家餐馆，或是与你的朋友们一块玩的时候，你就开始为你的"故

---

[2] adamant['ædəmənt] a. 坚定的，坚定不屈的
[3] constrain[kən'strein] vt. 强迫，限制，约束
[4] guru['guru:] n. （受下属崇敬的）领袖，头头

friends. That is, wherever you go, do firsthand observations on companies or products to gauge[5] whether the company is strong and growing. See for yourself whether the store is clean or messy. Are people lining up at the cash register or does the store look empty? Are the customers happy with the services or do they complain a lot? You are not likely to see an empty McDonalds or Wal-Mart.

On the playground, see what brand of soda your friends are drinking. Are most of them wearing Nike or Reebok shoes? Notice what new sports, such as roller hockey, have become popular. Then, look for companies that will benefit from the trend.

Also check with your parents, relatives, and neighbors who are doctors, engineers, and bankers. Your neighborhood doctor knows which companies make excellent drugs or the best medical equipment. Your engineer dad knows which companies have a dominant position in computer software or hardware. Your uncle banker knows which banks are the most profitable.

Once you begin to take notice of some of these companies, your next step is to learn more about the "story"of the company before you invest in it. You can learn more about the "story"

事"搜集信息。也就是说，不管你去哪里，搜集关于公司或产品的第一手的观察资料来判断这个公司是否很强，正在成长。你可以看这个商店是很干净还是很脏？顾客在收银机前排队交费还是这个商店看起来很空？顾客看起来对他们的服务是很满意还是都在抱怨？一般你是不可能看到一家空荡荡的麦当劳或沃尔玛的。

在操场上，看看你的朋友们都在喝什么牌子的苏打水，是不是大部分人都穿着耐克或锐步牌子的鞋，注意一下什么样的新的运动方式开始流行，如滚轴冰球。然后，去找那些有可能会从这种趋势中受益的公司。

还要跟你的那些职业是医生、工程师和银行家的父母、亲戚和邻居们联系。你的医生邻居知道哪家公司制的药最好，或者哪家公司的医疗设备最好。你的工程师父亲知道哪家公司在计算机软件或硬件方面处于统治地位。你的银行家叔叔知道哪些银行效益最好。

一旦你开始注意到这些公司，下一步就是在你投资之前，你要了解更多的关于"故事"的东西。你可以从商业杂志、年度报告和网络

---

[5] gauge[geidʒ] vt. 估计，判断

from resources such as trade magazines, annual reports, and the Internet. As the "story" goes on, you will want to know what must happen for the company to continue its growth spurts[6], as well as the pitfalls[7] that may slow its earnings.

Peter Lynch believes that, in the long run, there is a strong correlation[8] between the success of the company and the success of the stock. So look for the success stories. He further suggests that every few months, it is worthwhile to recheck the company's "story". That may involve checking the stores to see if there are still lines at the cash registers or new developments of the "story" from your neighbor's workplace. Also, check the earnings and growth from the company's quarterly reports or from the latest Value Line. As long as you own the stock, the "story" will never end.

As a young investor, you should start looking at the world through a stock picker's eyes. Better yet, you can collaborate with other kids across the Internet about your investment ideas.

等渠道了解这些。随着"故事"的发展，你还想知道如果公司继续保持增长势头会怎么样，当然，如果公司遇上意想不到的困难，就会影响收益。

彼得·林奇相信，长期来看，公司的成功和股票的成功有很密切的相互关系。所以要寻找成功的故事。他还建议每过几个月，我们应该去再次核查公司的"故事"。那也包括检查一下那些商店，看看是否还有那么多人在收银机前排队，或者是你邻居的工作单位的"故事"的新进展。也要从公司的季度报告或最新的行业标准中查查收益和增长。只要你持有这只股票，这个"故事"就永远不会结束。

作为一个年轻的投资者，你应该开始以一个选股者的眼睛来看这个世界。最好你还能通过互联网跟其他人交流你的投资理念。

---

6 spurt[spə:t] *n.* （短促或突然的爆发或）激增
7 pitfall['pitfɔ:l] *n.* 意想不到的困难，易犯的错误
8 correlation[ˌkɔri'leiʃən] *n.* 相互关系

1. Fidelity, 美国富达国际投资管理公司。美国富达投资集团成立于1946年，其创始人是爱德华 C. 约翰逊二世，总部设在美国波士顿。公司成立的最初承诺为，每天更加勤奋+更加机敏的工作，帮助小额投资者达到他们的目标。经过半个多世纪的发展，富达集团积累了丰富的投资管理经验，能够为客户提供便捷、专业的服务，而其规模也迅速扩大，已经由纯粹的共同基金公司发展成为一个多元化的金融服务公司，向客户提供包括基金管理、信托以及全球经纪服务在内的全方位服务。它是推出"货币市场共同基金账户"的第一家基金管理公司。富达集团拥有许多世界知名的基金经理，彼得·林奇就是其中最为出名的一个。

2. the Wharton School, 宾夕法尼亚大学沃顿商学院，被誉为现代MBA发源地。创立于1881年，是美国第一所大学商学院，也是世界上历史最悠久、学术声誉首屈一指的商学院。沃顿在各个主要经济专业领域的研究以及管理教育水平方面都有极高的声誉，在美国商学院各种排名中一直名列前茅。沃顿一直被认为是全美最具有开拓精神、创新意识和国际化视角的商学院。

宾夕法尼亚大学沃顿商学院

3. Magellan fund, 麦哲伦基金，该基金创立于1963年，原名富达国际基金(Fidelity International Fund),1965年3月更名为麦哲伦基金。富达·麦哲伦是美国共同基金业中的龙头，长期以来，它依靠良好的知名度和庞大的规模受到了广大投资者的青睐。这只基金最初由富达的总裁奈德·约翰逊管理，后来由彼得·林奇来操作。在林奇管理麦哲伦的13年中，年均收益率达29%，使业界极为震惊。

4. One Up on Wall Street, 《彼得·林奇的成功投资》，本书是投资者必备的国际畅销书。出版后的10年间，销量超过百万册，畅销全球。作者用浅显生动的语言娓娓道出了股票投资的诸多技巧。作者向广大的中小投资者提供了简单易学的投资分析方法，这些方法是作者多年的经验总结，具有很强的实践性，对于业余投资者来说尤为有益。

5. Beating the Street, 《战胜华尔街》，该书是彼得·林奇的经验之谈，没有空洞的说教，没有深奥的理论。身为基金经理，他没有大谈投资如何高深、神秘，没有劝告大家务必购买基金，反而开门见山地说"人人都该买股票"，并列举了中学生投资组合如何超越99%的基金业绩而创造的"圣·安吉利斯奇迹"；一万个民间投资俱乐部的投资业绩如何战胜华尔街四分之三的共同基金等。

6. roller hockey，滚轴冰球。

1. What is the importance of the two books written by Peter Lynch?
2. Peter's Cocktail Theory is quite famous, can you explain it?

平均每日成交额 average daily turnover

平仓交易 closing transaction

平价 parity value

母公司 parent company

永久债券 perpetual bond

申报期 reporting period

交付 delivery

交易大堂 trading floor; trading hall

交易日 trading day

交易商 dealer

交易费 trading fee

交易能力 trading capacity

全权委托账户 discretionary account

再贴现 rediscount

印花税 stamp duty

合约单位 contract unit

合资合同 joint venture contract

名义汇率 nominal exchange rate

吊销资格令 disqualification order

回本期 payoff period

Peter Lynch and His Cocktail Theory

彼得·林奇和他的
"鸡尾酒会理论"

Peter Lynch's *One Up On Wall Street* did not just talk about what we in general are better real estate investors. It talks about stocks too. However, before he goes deeper explaining the way he looks at stocks, he gracefully[9] shared in his book the four stages of stock market cycles which I found to be very useful. He called it the cocktail theory.

In the first stage of an upward market—one that has been down a while and that nobody expects to rise people aren't talking about stocks. In fact, if they lumber[10] up to ask me what I do for a living, and I answer, "I manage an equity[11] mutual fund", they nod politely and wander[12] away. If they don't wander away,then

彼得·林奇的书《彼得·林奇的成功投资》并不只是讨论我们通常是更好的房地产投资者。它也讨论股票。然而，在他进一步解释他是如何看待股票之前，他温文尔雅地在书里与读者共享股票市场周期的四个阶段，我认为非常有用。他把这个叫做"鸡尾酒会理论"。

在股市上升的第一阶段：在市场经过一段时间下跌之后，没有人期盼它能再次上涨时，人们都不谈论股市了。如果这时有人过来问我将怎样谋生，我会回答"试试买点普通的共同基金"。他们听完后会很有礼貌地点点头就走了。即使不走，他们也会很快把话题转到凯

---

9 gracefully['greisfuli] *ad.* 优美地，雅致地
10 lumber['lʌmbə] *vi.* 笨重地移动
11 equity['ekwiti] *n.* 普通股
12 wander['wɔndə] *vt.&vi.* 漫游，徘徊

they quickly change the subject to the Celtics game, the upcoming elections, or the weather. Soon they are talking to a nearby dentist about plaque[13]. When ten people would rather talk to dentist about plaque than to the manager of an equity mutual fund about stocks, it's likely that the market is about to turn up.

In stage two, after I confessed what I do for a living, the new acquaintances linger a bit longer perhaps long enough to tell me how risky the stock market is— before they move over to talk to the dentist. The cocktail party talk is still more about plaque than about stocks. The market's up 15% from stage one, but few paying attention.

In stage three, with the market up 30% from stage one, a crowd of interested parties ignores the dentist and circles around me all evening. A succession[14] of enthusiastic[15] individuals takes me aside to ask what stocks they should buy. Even the dentist is asking me what stocks he should buy. Everybody at the party has put money into one issue or another, and they're discussing what's happened.

In stage four, once again they're crowded around me but this time it's to tell me what

尔特人的游戏、即将进行的大选，或者天气情况之类。很快他们就会同旁边的一位牙医谈起有关治疗牙斑问题。当10个人宁愿与牙医谈论有关治疗牙斑的问题，而不愿意与一位基金经理谈论股市的时候，在林奇看来，股市极有可能出现转机了。

在第二阶段，当股市已经开始反弹上涨15%的时候，几乎没有人注意。林奇依然会告诉大家去买点基金。但新到的客人只会在去和牙医谈话之前，在林奇的身边多逗留一点时间，只是为了和他谈论一下股市有多大风险。鸡尾酒会上人们谈得更多的依然是治疗牙斑而不是股市。

到了第三个阶段，股市已经上升了30%，一大群兴致勃勃的人整晚都围在我身边，而忽视了牙医的存在。许多热情的客人把我叫到一边问我该买哪只股票，甚至牙医也这样问我。酒会上的每个人都把钱投在了这只或那只股票上，并且他们都在谈论股市的走势。

第四个阶段，所有客人都簇拥在我周围，但这一次是他们都来告

---

[13] plaque[plɑːk] *n.* （医）牙斑
[14] succession[sək'seʃən] *n.* 连续不断的人或事物
[15] enthusiastic[in,θjuːzi'æstik] *a.* 满腔热情的，热心的，极感兴趣的

stocks I should buy. Even the dentist has three or four tips, and in the next few days I look up his recommendations in the newspaper and they've all gone up. When the neighbors tell me what stocks to buy and then I wish I had taken their advice, it's sure sign that the market has reached a top and is due for a tumble[16]. said Lynch.

While Peter Lynch had explained the cocktail theory brilliantly, he does not believe in it to make his investment decision. Ultimately[17], he believes that undervalued stocks will rise while the most insanely[18] overvalued stock will fall, regardless of [19] where the market is.

诉我应该买哪只股票, 甚至是牙医也会给我推荐三五只股票, 在接下来的几天里, 我查了报上的那些牙医推荐的股票。这些股票确实都在上涨。但当邻居们都来告诉我应该买哪只股票时, 我希望我能听从他们的意见, 征兆已经很明确——股市已经达到高点并且是到了该下跌的时候了。林奇如是说。

当林奇兴致勃勃地解释"鸡尾酒会理论"的时候, 他并不完全相信并凭借这些来作出自己的投资决定。最后, 他相信, 不管是哪里的市场, 市值被低估的股票终会上涨, 而被过度高估的股票就会下跌。

非常点拨

　　1. Cocktail Theory, 在国外经常举办的鸡尾酒聚会上, 不同职业不同阶层的人们彼此相识, 聊天。彼得·林奇是世界上著名的基金经理, 他经手的基金市值曾经在13年内翻了29倍。在多年的投资经历中, 彼得·林奇经历过股市的大起大落, 在丰富的实践和经验中, 他总结出了著名的"鸡尾酒会理论", 即判断股市走势的四个阶段。

---

[16] tumble['tʌmbl] *n*. 摔倒, 坠落
[17] ultimately['ʌltimitli] *ad*. 最后, 最终
[18] insanely[in'seinli] *ad*. 疯狂的, 狂暴地
[19] regardless of 不管, 不顾

Lin Yifu

Unit 14

Lin Yifu
世界银行副行长：林毅夫

主题札记

"军人的理想是马革裹尸还，我最大的愿望就是累死在书桌上。"

这是当代中国著名的经济学家林毅夫的一句名言。今时，林毅夫已前往世界银行，告别了他在北京大学中国经济研究中心主任、教授和博士生导师的身份。

林毅夫是著名经济学家。曾是第7届、第8届和第9届全国政协委员，曾任北京大学中国经济研究中心主任、教授和博士生导师。世界银行首席经济学家兼负责发展经济学的高级副行长。

2008年2月4日，世界银行行长罗伯特·佐利克（Robert Zoellick）正式任命北京大学经济学教授林毅夫为世行首席经济学家兼负责发展经济学的高级副行长。世行的首席经济学家在拟定研究计划及发展方向上扮演着相当重要的决策角色，林毅夫出任世行首席经济学家将进一步转变世行与中国的关系。林毅夫是首位在世界银行或国际货币基金组织获得如此高职位的中国人。

阅读长廊

World Bank appoint to strengthen Beijing Ties

世界银行的此次任命将加强与中国政府的联系

Professor Lin Yifu is a Chinese economist and incumbent Chief Economist of the World Bank. He is also professor and founding director of the China Centre for Economic Research (CCER) at Peking University.

林毅夫教授是中国经济学家，也是世界银行现任首席经济学家。他也是北京大学教授，中国经济研究中心主任。

Prof. Lin gained a Ph.D. at the University of Chicago in 1986 and has twice been awarded China's top economics honour, the Sun Yefang Prize, in 1993 and 2001.

林毅夫教授1986年在芝加哥大学获得博士学位，并于1993年和2001年两次获得中国经济学最高荣誉——孙冶方经济科学奖。

But Prof. Lin is just as well known for his own extraordinary personal history as he is for his professional achievements.

不过，林毅夫非凡的个人经历也与他在专业上的成就一样富有盛名。

Prof. Lin defected[1] from Taiwan in 1979, when stationed as a soldier on the heavily fortified island of Kinmen, just off the coast of China, near Fujian province.

林毅夫于1979年逃离台湾。当时，他是一名台湾士兵，驻扎在重兵防守的金门岛。金门岛就在中国大陆海岸线附近，临近福建省。

---

[1] defect [di'fekt] *vi.* 逃跑，开小差，背叛

Most famously, Prof. Lin, according to the story he himself has told friends, swam from Taiwan to reach the mainland.

At the time, he left behind his wife and child who were living in Taiwan. They were later reunited when Lin went to study in the United States. While an officer in the Taiwan Army, Lin was held up as a model soldier for choosing to be in the army. Lin was considered as a "superstar" officer. Taiwan originally listing him as missing but in 2000 issued an order for his arrest on charges of desertion.

Dr. Lin founded the China Center for Economic Research (CCER) at Peking University with some other scholars in 1994. CCER gathers the most Chinese economic scholars with solid education background from abroad and it is well established in the world.

He was one of the first PRC citizens to receive a Ph.D. in economics from a US university, and is a leading Chinese economist; he serves as a consultant[2] to major international organizations, and is on the editorial board of several international academic economics journals.

He has been included in *Who's Who in the World* and other various Who's Whos. His major teaching and research areas are Economic

最著名的情节是，据林毅夫本人对朋友讲，他是从金门岛游到大陆的。

当时，他把妻子和孩子留在了台湾。后来在林毅夫去美国学习后，他的妻儿才得以和他团聚。当年他在台湾军队的时候，林毅夫因为选择留在军队而被当做模范战士。他被人们认为是"超级明星"军官。台湾开始把他列为失踪人员，但是在2000年，发布了一项逮捕他的命令，指控他逃跑。

1994年，林博士和一些学者们一起在北京大学创立了中国经济研究中心。中国经济研究中心聚集了大部分从海外学成回国的有扎实的教育背景的经济领域学者。

他是最早在美国大学获得经济学博士学位的中国公民之一，是首位中国经济学家。他是很多重要国际组织的顾问，也是好几份国际经济学术期刊的编委。

他被收进《世界名人录》和其他各种名人录。他主要的教学和研究领域是中国的经济发展，中国的

---

[2] consultant[kən'sʌltənt] *n.* 顾问

Development in China, Economic Reform in China, Innovation and Change, Agricultural Economics, and Development Economics. He is vice Chairman of Committee for Economic Affairs of Chinese People's Political Consultative[3] Conference.

He received his Ph.D. in economics from the University of Chicago in 1986 and is the author of 16 books, including *The China Miracle: Development Strategy and Economic Reform*, which has been published in seven languages, and *State-owned Enterprise Reform in China*, which is available in Chinese, Japanese, and English. He has published more than 100 articles in international journals and collected volumes on history, development, and transition.

According to the latest news, the World Bank will appoint a Chinese economist to a senior position in a move that will buttress[4] the institution's ties with Beijing and lift the profile of developing countries.

Lin Yifu, or Justin Lin, is expected to be appointed as the organisation's chief economist, according to bank officials quoted by agencies and *the Wall Street Journal*.

Prof. Lin is one of China's leading economists,

经济改革、创新和变化，农业经济学和发展经济学。他还是中国人民政治协商会议经济事务委员会副主席。

1986年他在美国芝加哥大学获得经济学博士学位，并著有16本书，包括：《中国的奇迹：发展战略与经济改革》（以7种语言出版）和《中国的国有企业改革》（有中文、日文和英文版）。他在一些有关历史、发展和过渡的国际刊物和合集上发表过100多篇文章。

根据最新消息，世界银行将任命一位中国经济学家担任要职，此举将加强世行与中国政府的联系，并将提高发展中国家的地位。

据各通讯社和《华尔街日报》援引的世行官员的话，预计世行将任命林毅夫为首席经济学家。

林毅夫是中国最著名的经济学

---

[3] consultative[kən'sʌltətiv] *a.* 商议的，顾问的
[4] buttress['bʌtris] *v.* 支撑，加固

as the head of a think-tank[5] at Peking University and an adviser to the central government.

Highly respected as an economist, his appointment will also strengthen Beijing's ties to the World Bank.

The World Bank is trying to refurbish[6] its relations with China, joining it as a development partner in Africa and trying to attract more Chinese to work with it in Washington and elsewhere.

Prof. Lin has written extensively on China's famine[7] during the "Great Leap Forward" in the early 1960s, and more recently was instrumental in shaping Beijing's new policy to reinvigorate the rural economy.

The so-called "New Socialist Countryside" policy was the centrepiece of the government's economic programme announced at the annual session of China's parliament in 2006.

His recent research has focused the continuing role of the state in China's economy, and the potential challenge its success poses to conventional theories about the greater efficiencies of the private sector.

家之一，是北京大学一个智囊机构的负责人，也是中央政府的顾问。

作为一名备受尊敬的经济学家，他的这项任命也会加强中国政府与世行的联系。

世行正努力与中国重修旧好，吸收其成为世行在非洲的一个发展伙伴，并努力吸引更多的中国人到华盛顿等地为世行工作。

林毅夫撰写了大量关于20世纪60年代"大跃进"时期中国饥荒的文章。最近，在中国政府制定振兴农村经济的新政策的过程中，他也发挥了很大作用。

所谓的"社会主义新农村"政策，是中国政府2006年在全国人民代表大会上宣布的经济计划的中心内容。

他最近的研究重点是国家在中国经济中的持续作用，以及中国政府的成功对"私营领域效率更高"的传统理论构成的潜在挑战。

---

[5] think-tank *n.* 智囊团，智囊机构
[6] refurbish [ˌriːˈfəːbiʃ] *vt.* 刷新，擦亮
[7] famine [ˈfæmin] *n.* 饥荒

财经宝库

1. the China Centre for Economic Research (CCER)，北京
大学中国经济研究中心（英文简称为CCER）创办于1994年
8月，是集研究、教学和培训于一体的学术机构，2004年当
选为"教育部人文社会科学百所重点基地"。中心的建立是
北京大学进行教学和科研体制改革的一种新探索，也是吸引
海外留学人员回国服务的一种开创性尝试。目的在于动员各
界资源，聚集一批杰出中青年经济学、管理学者，为北京大
学的教学科研、为中国经济改革和发展、为当代经济学、管

北京大学中国经济研究中心

理学理论的研究作出贡献。该中心直属北京大学，实行学校和董事会领导下的主任负责
制，林毅夫教授曾担任中心主任。

2. *Who's Who in the World*，《世界名人录》，是世界上第一套大型人物辞书，该书的
出版能加强世界各国、各地区和各民族人民之间的交流与合作。

3. *The China Miracle: Development Strategy and Economic Reform*，《中国的奇迹：
发展战略与经济改革》，经过五六年的仔细观察和认真思考以及一年多埋头写作，林毅
夫、蔡方、李周三位学者出版了他们的著作《中国的奇迹：发展战略与经济改革》，提
出和讨论的是有关经济发展、国家兴衰的重大论题。特别是在目前情况下，中国是世界
上经济增长最快的国家之一，世界各国和很多大的跨国公司都看好中国，中国的改革也
取得了巨大的成功，创造了向市场经济转型的所谓"中国模式"。

4. the University of Chicago，芝加哥大学，是一所私立、男女同校、无宗教派别的综
合性大学，1891年由约翰·洛克菲勒创办，1892年10月1日正式开课。芝加哥大学的校
训译成中文是"益智厚生"，意思是"提升知识，以充实人生"。该大学对教育观念的
"宏观"与实验精神，奠定了它在美国教育史上的重要地位；而它在学术研究上的地位
与贡献，也同样值得称道。

5. the Sun Yefang Prize, 孙冶方经济科学奖是为纪念我国卓越的经济学家孙冶方同志对经济科学的重大贡献，表彰和奖励对经济科学作出突出贡献的集体和个人，推动中国经济科学的繁荣和发展而设立的。孙冶方经济科学奖于1985年开始设立和评选，每两年评选、颁发一次，是迄今为止中国经济学界的最高奖。

6. Kinmen, 金门，位于厦门湾口，它由大金门与小金门等12个小岛组成，岛屿面积147平方公里，居民约5万人。

DIY工作室

1. Why did Dr. Lin found the China Center for Economic Research (CCER) at Peking University?

2. Why did he swim from Taiwan to the mainland?

归类记忆卡片

一级市场 primary market	少数股东权益 minority interest
内部储备 inner reserve	公开谴责 public censure
内幕交易 insider dealing	反通货膨胀 disinflation
公平市值 fair market value	公开售股 open offer
公开招股 offer to the public	公众持股市值 public float capitalisation
公开认购 offer for subscription	公司仓 house position; firm position

公积金计划 provident fund scheme
分销 distribution
内资股（中国内地）domestic share
(Mainland China)
引伸波幅 implied volatility

午市 afternoon session
反弹 rally
公司交易板（英国）Company Bulletin
Board(UK)
文件风险 documentation risk

World Bank Chief Economist Professor Justin Yifu Lin to Speak at CUHK on 31 March

The Chinese University of Hong Kong (CUHK) has invited Professor Justin Yifu Lin, Senior Vice President and Chief Economist of the World Bank, to present a public lecture on "Development and Transition[8]: Idea, Strategy and Viability[9]" on campus on 31 March 2008.

世界银行首席经济学家林毅夫三月三十一日于香港中文大学演讲

香港中文大学（以下简称中大）邀得世界银行高级副行长兼首席经济学家林毅夫教授于3月31日在中大校园主持公开讲座，以《发展与转型：思潮、战略和自生能力》为题，与中大师生、校友及政商界人士分享其真知灼见。

---

[8] transition [træn'ziʃ ən] *n.* 过渡，转变，变迁
[9] viability [ˌvaiə'biliti] *n.* 生存能力，发展能力

Professor Lin is the first Chief Economist of the World Bank from a developing country, and the first Chinese assuming this position. Being an expert on economic development and particularly agriculture, Professor Lin plays a crucial role in advising the World Bank on developing world issues.

In the coming lecture, Professor Justin Lin will share his scholarship with CUHK staff, students, alumni[10] and members of the political and commercial sectors. He will analyse why the dominant social thinking about the modernization of developing countries in the 1950s and their transition in the 1990s was incorrect, and how they shaped government policies and established institutions in the developing countries. Professor Lin will also discuss why the governments of a few economies in East Asia managed to escape the influence of the dominant social thinking in the 1950s, and why China and Vietnam did not follow the transitional approach advocated by the dominant social thinking in the 1980s.

The lecture will be broadcast live to local universities, CUHK Tung Wah Group of Hospitals Community College and Hong Kong Science and Technology Parks, as well as Peking, Fudan,

林毅夫教授是世界银行第一位来自发展中国家的首席经济学家，亦是首位华人出任此职。作为经济发展尤其是农业方面的专家，林教授将会在世界银行中担当要职，就发展中国家的经济发展提供专业意见。

在接下来的讲座中，林教授将和中大的教师、学生、校友以及政治、商务部门的人士分享他的学识。就发展中国家在20世纪50年代的现代化及20世纪90年代的经济转型，分析过往不正确的主导社会观念，并解释有关观念如何影响发展中国家的政府决策及既定制度。林教授亦会探讨为何少数东亚国家的政府没有受到20世纪50年代主流社会观念的影响，以及中国和越南为何不跟随20世纪80年代盛行的经济转型理念。

为了让更多市民有机会聆听林教授的演说，大会特别安排讲座直播至香港多所大学，香港中文大学（东华三院小区书院）、香港科技

---

[10] alumni[əˈlʌmnai] n. (复) 校友，毕业生

Shanghai Jiao Tong, Tsinghua, Zhejiang, Nanjing and Sun Yat-sen Universities on the mainland. It will also be available on the Hong Kong Education City web site. The broadcast is intended to promote academic exchange and allow more people to benefit from the lecture.

Professor Lin is Professor and Founding Director of the China Centre for Economic Research (CCER) at Peking University. Among many of his public roles in China, Professor Lin is Vice Chairman, Committee for Economic Affairs of the Chinese People's Political Consultation Conference and Vice Chairman of the All-China Federation of Industry and Commerce. He is representative of the Eleventh National People's Congress. He also serves on several national and international committees, leading groups, and councils on development policy, technology, and the environment.

园，以及多所内地著名学府，包括北京大学、复旦大学、上海交通大学、清华大学、浙江大学、南京大学及中山大学。从香港教育城网站上也可聆听林教授的演讲。广播是为了促进学术交流，使更多的人能够从中受益。

林教授创立北京大学中国经济研究中心，并担任主任至今。他在中国担任多项公职，包括全国政协经济委员会副主任、中华全国工商业联合会副主席，现为第十一届全国人大代表，并是多个国内和国际有关发展政策、科技和环境的委员会、领导小组和协会的成员。

190

非常点拨

1. The Chinese University of Hong Kong (CUHK)，香港中文大学（简称中大），成立于1963年，是香港成立的第二所大学，亦是香港八所受香港大学教育资助委员会资助并可颁授学位的高等教育院校之一。当年政府为推广中文教育，特意成立一所以中文为主要授课语言、中英双语并重的大学，并拨出沙田马料水一个山头以供建校。它的校园面积为香港最大。

香港中文大学

Sanford Weill

Unit 15